Fundamental Canadian Payroll Administration

Author:

Carina Casuga

2024 Edition

Fundamental Canadian Payroll Administration

Contents

LEARNING OUTCOMES

This handbook serves as a guide to learning fundamental Canadian payroll administration.

Learning Outcomes:

- Understand legislative compliance requirements in relation to payroll.

- Learn how to calculate gross pay to net pay.

- Understand the various types of employment income and taxation related to the income.

- Understand various types of payroll forms and records.

- Understand the importance of documentation of all payroll activities.

- Comprehend the roles of Canada's governing bodies.

- Understand federal and provincial legislation relating to employment functions.

- Ability to produce pay related records and calculations that vary in complexity.

- Understand month end and year end reporting requirements.

- Understand and commit to essential confidentiality and professional ethics.

- Appreciate the value of payroll as a profession.

About the Author
Carina Cheng Casuga

Experience

Manager, Global Payroll and Benefits

Instructor, Payroll Administration – Langara College

Author, Fundamental Canadian Payroll Administration

Coach, Personal and Professional Development

Mentor, National Payroll Institute (NPI)

Implementation Specialist, Payroll and Benefits

Volunteer, Subject Matter Expert (SME) NPI

Board member, Richmond Pentecostal Church

Education:

Certified Payroll Leadership Professional (PLP) – NPI - Canada

Certified Payroll Professional (CPP) – American Payroll Association (APA)

Certified, Mental Health First Aid – Mental Health Commission of Canada

Certified, Personal & Executive Coach – Coaching & Positive Psychology Institute

Certified, Global Payroll Management - Global Payroll Management Institute

Certifiied, Leadership Development – University of British Columbia, Sauder

Diploma - Business Management Diploma - Richmond District College

Bachelor of Science in Medical Technology - Saint Louis University (SLU), Philippines

Fundamental Canadian Payroll Administration

- Over 20 years payroll and benefits experience in a wide variety of industries (i.e. Transportation, Tourism, Wealth Management, Manufacturing) responsible for managing payments and benefits of up to 1,500 global employees, salary, hourly, commission, union, and non-union payrolls.

- Over 12 years' payroll and benefits management experience, working with large complex Human Capital Management (HCM) encompassing payroll and benefits system management, implementation, change management, optimizing business processes using Ceridian, ADP and UKG

- Completed and contributed to the following projects:
    - Development of Total Rewards Statements (TRS),
    - Group Benefits Open Enrollment and Benefit Enhancements
    - Group Benefits contract renewals and proposals
    - Vendor selection and management – HRIS, Payroll, Group Benefits
    - Workflow development, continuous process improvements
    - Payroll & group benefits process documentation and guides
    - Corporate employee policy development
    - Total Wellness Programs – Health Challenge, Lunch and Learns, Flu Clinics

- System implementation ADP Pay@Work to UKG, ADP Pay@Work to Ceridian (HPL), UK Pension Change, Expense Reimbursement to Payroll

- Lead global teams to increase efficiency via coaching, mentoring, training, resource planning, and performance management. Relationship management and collaboration with stake holders

Disclaimer:

1. General Information

This book offers general information on selected topics on pay, employment, legislation and compliance as it relates to payroll.

2. Not Legal Advice

It is crucial to note that this content is not to be construed as legal advice and is not intended to replace applicable employment and taxation laws.

3. No Substitute for Legal Counsel

This book should not be relied upon as a substitute for professional legal counsel in specific situations. For personalized advice, it is highly recommended that you seek legal guidance or consult a qualified tax accountant.

4. Consultation Encourage

While efforts have been made to ensure the information is current, it is advisable to seek legal advice or consult a tax accountant to address individual circumstances.

5. For Reference Only

It is important to recognize that, despite our efforts to provide up-to-date information, government legislation always takes precedence.

1. INTRODUCTION

What is Payroll?

Payroll is the business process of paying employees, calculating and distribution of wages and taxes. For some companies, it is the highest expense for a company. It is the compensation a company must pay to its employees for a set period and on a given date. Payroll can also be referred to as a list of a company's employees and the amount of compensation due to each of them.

Payroll is essential to the long-term health of every business, the financial wellness of workers and the strength of our economy — all of whom rely on our members to ensure the timely and accurate annual payment of $1.059 trillion in wages and taxable benefits, and $364 billion in statutory remittances.

Payroll staff usually reports to either the Finance or Human Resources department of a company. Some companies outsourced to specialized firms that handle paycheck processing, employee benefits, insurance, tax withholding and remittance and reporting i.e. Ceridian, ADP, UKG, Payroll Guardian

The payroll process can include tracking hours worked for employees, calculating pay, and distributing payments via direct deposit or cheque. Calculating payroll involves many components and can be complex. Components of payroll includes Gross pay, Deductions, Taxes, Wage Garnishments and Net Pay.

Reference:

> https://payroll.ca/who-we-are
>
> https://www.investopedia.com/terms/p/payroll.asp

Payroll Administration

Payroll Administration encompasses all the tasks involved in paying an organization's employees. It typically involves keeping track of hours worked and ensuring employees receive the appropriate amount of pay. It also includes calculating taxes and ensuring the remittances are properly withheld and processed.

Depending on the company, a range of other deductions may be calculated and distributed as part of the payroll administration process. The specific tasks involved in payroll administration tend to vary according to the needs of each unique company or organization.

Handling payroll-related problems is part of payroll administration as well. If an employee is paid an incorrect amount or a payment fails to go through, both things are issues dealt with by this department. Likewise, tax filing and deduction errors are payroll matters as well.

Payroll administration may be very simple, involving the payment of just a handful of employees, or very complicated, involving payroll for thousands of employees. In some small companies, it may be handled by the owner of the company or an employee. However, other companies may have many employees to pay and keep track of, necessitating a well-planned, efficient system.

Some companies choose to handle these tasks in-house, often creating a separate department just for the handling of payroll. Such organizations purchase software to streamline payroll-related tasks. Some companies even have special software designed for them, creating a system that is tailored to their unique requirements.

Many companies decide to outsource payroll administration to other companies that handle most, if not all, payroll-related tasks for the companies they serve. Some also provide management and human resource assistance as well. Many tailor their services to meet the needs of organizations of all sizes and types. Some even offer on-site help and payroll consultations as well.

Payroll Administrator

A payroll administrator handles all matters that relate to the payment of salaries and wages to the staff of an organization.

The administrator is responsible for calculating, deducting, and processing of taxes and other benefits that are offered to employees by an organization or company.

As such, a payroll administrator is the first point of contact regarding employee time and attendance, payments and employee pay history.

Depending on the size of the company or organization, a payroll administrator's task would involve the issuance of cheques for weekly, biweekly, and monthly payments, and the job could be as complex as involving the payment to thousands of employees and contractors.

The payroll administrator may handle managing direct deposits, benefits, withholding payroll deductions, paid leave, sick time reporting and the monitoring of employees' hour compliance.

The information a Payroll Administrator manages affects employee compensation, employee benefits, employer financials, government entities, third parties, and employee financials and engagement. The payroll administrator is the gatekeeper for confidential information.

Payroll Compensation

Based on Government of Canada Job Bank a Payroll Administrator can be paid between $19.00 to $33.90 per hour in British Columbia or between $29.96 to $43.65 in Northwest Territories.

Reference: https://www.investopedia.com/terms/p/payroll.asp

Salary Guide

Reference:

https://www.roberthalf.ca/en/salary-guide

https://www.randstad.ca/salaries/salary-guide/

Payroll Stakeholders:

Duties and Responsibilities

- Maintain and update employee information, such as records of employee attendance, leave and overtime to calculate pay and benefit entitlements, in Canadian and other currencies, using manual or computerized systems.
- Prepare and verify statements of earnings for employees, indicating gross and net salaries and deductions such as taxes, union dues, garnishments and insurance and pension plans.
- Prepare, verify and process all employee payroll related payments, including regular pay, benefit payments, and special payments such as bonuses and vacation pay.
- Complete, verify and process forms and documentation for administration of benefits such as pension plans, leaves, share savings, employment and medical insurance.
- Prepare payroll related filings and supporting documentation, such as year-end tax statements, pension, Records of Employment and other statements.
- Provide information on payroll matters, benefit plans and collective agreement provisions.
- Compile, review, and monitor statistical reports, statements, and summaries related to pay and benefits accounts.
- Prepare and balance period-end reports and reconcile issued payrolls to bank statements.
- Identify and resolve payroll discrepancies.
- May be responsible for the development or implementation of payroll policies, procedures, or processes.

Reference:

https://www.jobbank.gc.ca/marketreport/occupation/25792/ca;jsessionid=743D2347AF58A51B1 76E8BE2112B1579.jobsearch76

Employer Responsibilities:

You are acting as a representative of the company. You are responsible for deducting, remitting, and reporting payroll deductions. You also have responsibilities in situations such as hiring an employee when an employee leaves or if the business ceases its operations.

The following are the responsibilities of the employer and, in some circumstances, the trustee and payer:

- Open and maintain a payroll program account.
- Get your employee's social insurance number (SIN). Every employee must give you their SIN to work in Canada.
- Get a completed federal Form TD1, Personal Tax Credits Return, and, if applicable, a provincial or territorial Form TD1. New employees or recipients of other amounts such as pension income must fill out this form.
- Deduct CPP contributions, EI premiums, and income tax from remuneration or other amounts, including taxable benefits and allowances, you pay in a pay period. You should hold these amounts in trust for the Receiver General and keep them separate from the operating funds of your business. Make sure these amounts are not part of an estate in liquidation, assignment, receivership, or bankruptcy.
- Remit these deductions along with your share of CPP contributions and EI premiums.
- Report the employee's income and deductions on the appropriate T4 or T4A slip. You must file an information return on or before the last day of February of the following calendar year.
- Prepare a Record of Employment (ROE) when an employee stop working and has an interruption of earnings.
- Keeping records of what you do because our officers can ask to see them.

*Reference:

T4001 Employers Guide – Payroll Deductions and Remittances

https://www.canada.ca/en/revenue-agency/services/forms-publications/publications/t4001/employers-guide-payroll-deductions-remittances.html#P263_15329

2. EMPLOYMENT

Keeping Records

CRA requires companies to keep your paper and electronic records for at least six years after the year to which they relate. If you want to destroy them before the six-year period is over, fill out Form T137, Request for Destruction of Records, and send it to your tax services office.

- Six (6) years - Keep paper and electronic records.

- Form T137 – Request for Destruction of Records – before 6 years

   Reference:
   https://www.canada.ca/en/revenue-agency/services/tax/businesses/topics/keeping-records.html

BC Payroll Records

- Must be in English.

- Be kept at employer's principal place of business in British Columbia

- Retained by the employer for 4 years after the date on which the payroll records were created.

- In the absence of payroll records – Employee records will be considered for the purpose of calculating outstanding wages

Reference:

https://www2.gov.bc.ca/gov/content/employment-business/employment-standards-advice/employment-standards/forms-resources/igm/esa-part-3-section-28

Information Required – BC

Jurisdiction	Information Required for Each Employee		Length of Time
British Columbia	• Name • Address • Date of birth • Occupation • Telephone number • Date of beginning of employment • Hours of work • Hours per day • Overtime hours • Wage rate • Gross wages • Net wages • Nature and amount of deductions • Date wages were paid • Work period corresponding to the payment • Nature and amount of bonus, premiums, allowances, commissions and other payments	• Vacation reference year, dates and duration of vacation • Date and amount of vacation pay • Statutory holiday pay • Date of compensatory holiday • Date of notice of termination • Date employment ends • Amount in lieu of notice • Amount in lieu of vacation • Banked time, dates and remaining amounts in the bank • The benefits paid to the employee • Payroll records must be in English	4 years after the date on which the payroll records were created

Employee and Employer Relationship

- In general, it is when a worker agrees to work for an employer for a period in exchange for paid compensation.

  - The employee retains the right to be recalled for work.
  - There is an expectation of work to be performed by the employee.
  - The employee continues to accrue benefits in the organization's pension plan.
  - The employees continue to participate in all the benefit plans that were available while they were employed.

Reference:
https://www.canada.ca/en/revenue-agency/services/forms-publications/publications/rc4110/employee-self-employed.html

Employee vs Contractor

ESA does not apply to an independent contractor, as they are self-employed. The facts of the working relationship determines the employment status.

	Employee	Independent Contractor
Number of Employer(s)	Usually only has one employer	Usually consults for more than one company
Work Hours	Set by employer	Set by contractor him/herself
Place of Work	Usually, employer's office	Works out of his/her own home
Benefits	Can receive employment benefits, such as insurance, from employer Entitled to workers' comp and unemployment compensation	Does not receive employment benefits from employer Not eligible for workers' comp or unemployment comp
Control	Works under control of employer	Works independently
Work	Does as is directed by employer	Decides how to accomplish tasks without employer's input
Taxes	Some taxes on wages withheld by employer	Not subject to tax withholdings pays self-employment tax
Termination	Can be terminated by employer only for good cause and with notice (unless "at will")	Usually, can be terminated by employer for any reason at any time (unless contract states otherwise)
Wages & Hours	Covered by federal and state wage and hour laws (i.e., minimum wage and overtime)	Paid according to contract. Does not receive overtime pay

More information can be found by visiting CRA

Social Insurance Number (SIN)

A Social Insurance Number (SIN) is a nine-digit number that allows Canadian citizens, permanent residents, or temporary residents of Canada to legally work and receive benefits and services from the government.

A SIN can only be used by one person, and should not be used as identification, or on application forms, and should always be kept in a safe place.

Employers require a new employee's SIN within 3 days of being hired. If the newly hired employee does not provide this number, they are considered not legally entitled to work in Canada.

The employer must notify Service Canada within 6 days, and the employer risks being fined $100 if no reasonable effort was documented to retrieve this information.

SINs that begin with a "9" carry are issued to workers who are neither Canadian citizens nor permanent residents. They are temporary and are valid until the expiry date as indicated on the authorizing immigration document.

SIN beginning with a "9"

Ensure that all employees who have a SIN beginning with a "9" are authorized to work in Canada and that their immigration document has not expired.

SINs beginning with a "9" are issued to temporary workers who are neither Canadian citizens nor permanent residents. These temporary SINs are valid until the expiry date indicated on the immigration document authorizing them to work in Canada.

Ask to see the employee's existing immigration document authorizing him or her to work in Canada (e.g. work permit, study permit) and verify that it has not expired. If the immigration document has expired, ask the employee to contact Immigration, Refugees and Citizenship Canada (IRCC) to obtain a valid document and to provide it to Service Canada to have the new expiry date entered into their SIN record

For more information about hiring or extending the work of temporary foreign workers, visit IRCC's Hire foreign workers page or contact the IRCC Call Centre at 1-888-242-2100.

Fundamental Canadian Payroll Administration

Your key responsibilities regarding SIN

Request each new employee's SIN within three (3) days after the day on which their employment begins.

- Correctly identify employees with the help of pieces of identification before finalizing their employment documents.
- Ensure that employees have a valid SIN. This number is used to administer government benefits under the Income Tax Act, the Canada Pension Plan Act and the Employment Insurance Act.
- If a new employee does not have a SIN and is eligible to work in Canada, instruct the employee to apply for a SIN at a Service Canada office. If the employee's application and identity document(s) are in order, he or she will receive a SIN in one visit.
- You can confirm the SIN of a current or former employee by contacting Service Canada at 1-866-274-6627. If calling from outside Canada, dial 506-548-7961 (long distance charges apply). You will need to provide your business number issued by Canada Revenue Agency, along with necessary information to verify the identity of your company as well as the employee.

For more information about hiring a foreign student,

*Reference:

https://www.canada.ca/en/employment-social-development/programs/ei/ei-list/ei-employers-sin.html

https://www.canada.ca/en/employment-social-development/services/sin/qualify.html

Contact Immigration, Refugees and Citizenship Canada - Canada.ca

visit IRCC's Hire international students page.

Canada's Legislative Governing Bodies:

Federal and Provincial Governments

Governing Legislative Bodies in Canada

Federal Agencies	Provincial – Employment Standards
	Alberta
	British Columbia
Canada Labour Code	Manitoba
	New Brunswick
	Newfoundland and Labrador
Canada Revenue Agency	Northwest Territories
	Nova Scotia
	Nunavut
Service Canada	Ontario
	Prince Edward Island
	Québec
	Saskatchewan
	Yukon Territory

Employment Standards

Each province legislates its employment standards, and the Government of Canada defines the *Canada Labour Code* as federal labour standards for federally regulated businesses.

The **Canada Revenue Agency (CRA)** administers tax laws for the Government of Canada and for most provinces and territories and administers various social and economic benefit and incentive programs delivered through the tax system.

Service Canada provides Canadians with a single point of access to a wide range of government services and benefits.

Employment Standards BC

The laws in British Columbia set standards for payment, compensation, and working conditions in most workplaces. The standards promote open communication, fair treatment, and work-life balance for employees.

These are defined in the **Employment Standards Act (ESA).**

Not every work issue is related to BC employment standards.

Not all workers classified as employees are covered by the Employment Standards Act.

Type of Work Limited or Excluded from ESA:

- Managers
- Election Workers
- Farm Workers
- Foster Parents
- Student Nurses

Workers Not Covered Under the ESA:

- Unionized Workplaces
- Independent Contractors
- Professionals

New Employee Information

Information necessary to pay an employee.

• Legal Name	• Start Date – End Date if applicable
• Address	• Hours of Work
• Date of Birth	• Pay Frequency
• Social Insurance Number (SIN)	• Rate of Pay
• Bank Account for EFT payments	• Province/Territory of Employment
• Pension Plan Enrollment	• Personal Tax Credits – TD1 Federal and Provincial
• Benefits Enrollment Data	• Union Membership

Hiring Employees in BC – **ESA – BC**

New Employee Checklist – National Payroll Institute (NPI)

Reference:

https://payroll.ca/payroll-guidelines?page=2

https://www2.gov.bc.ca/gov/content/employment-business/employment-standards-advice/employment-standards/hiring

Minimum Wage

Employees must be paid at least minimum wage.

The minimum wage in B.C. is currently **$17.40** per hour (as of June 1, 2024).

- **June 1, 2024 - $17.40 per hour**
- June 1, 2023 – $16.75 per hour
- June 1, 2022 – $15.65 per hour
- June 1, 2021 – $15.20 per hour
- June 1, 2020 – $14.60 per hour
- June 1, 2019 – $13.85 per hour
- June 1, 2018 – $12.65 per hour

Minimum wage applies regardless of how employees are paid – hourly, salary, commission or on an incentive basis. If an employee's wage is below minimum wage for the hours they worked, the employer must top up their payment so that it's equal to minimum wage.

Reference
https://www2.gov.bc.ca/gov/content/employment-business/employment-standards-advice/employment-standards/wages/minimum-wage

The hourly minimum wage is different for each province or territory across Canada.

Reference - Retail Council Link

The Canadian Payroll Association offers video overview on

Understanding Your Pay.

Reference:

https://www.youtube.com/watch?v=lH4a2_aY4po

TD1 – Tax Credits Return

- The TD1 Personal Tax Credit Returns are used to determine the amount of tax to be deducted from an individual's employment income or other income.
- Responsibility of the Employer to request completed TD1 form from each new employee.
- Responsibility of the Employee to provide updated form to the employer if changes in personal circumstances.
- If a TD1 form is not available, the basic personal amount is applied in their TD1 calculation.

Payroll Administrators are **responsible** for the following:
• Maintain payroll program account
• Social Insurance Number
• Completed TD1 Federal and Pprovincial form
• Keep records

Fundamental Canadian Payroll Administration

Canada Revenue Agency Agence du revenu du Canada	**2024 Personal Tax Credits Return**	**Protected B** when completed

TD1

Read page 2 before filling out this form. Your employer or payer will use this form to determine the amount of your tax deductions.

Fill out this form based on the best estimate of your circumstances.

If you do not fill out this form, your tax deductions will only include the basic personal amount, estimated by your employer or payer based on the income they pay you.

Last name	First name and initial(s)	Date of birth (YYYY/MM/DD)	Employee number

Address	Postal code	For non-residents only Country of permanent residence	Social insurance number

1. Basic personal amount – Every resident of Canada can enter a basic personal amount of $15,705. However, if your net income from all sources will be greater than $173,205 and you enter $15,705, you may have an amount owing on your income tax and benefit return at the end of the tax year. If your income from all sources will be greater than $173,205 you have the option to calculate a partial claim. To do so, fill in the appropriate section of Form TD1-WS, Worksheet for the 2024 Personal Tax Credits Return, and enter the calculated amount here. **15,705**

2. Canada caregiver amount for infirm children under age 18 – Only one parent may claim $2,616 for each infirm child born in 2007 or later who lives with both parents throughout the year. If the child does not live with both parents throughout the year, the parent who has the right to claim the "Amount for an eligible dependant" on line 8 may also claim the Canada caregiver amount for the child.

3. Age amount – If you will be 65 or older on December 31, 2024, and your net income for the year from all sources will be $44,325 or less, enter $8,790. You may enter a partial amount if your net income for the year will be between $44,325 and $102,925. To calculate a partial amount, fill out the line 3 section of Form TD1-WS.

4. Pension income amount – If you will receive regular pension payments from a pension plan or fund (not including Canada Pension Plan, Quebec Pension Plan, old age security, or guaranteed income supplement payments), enter **whichever is less**: $2,000 or your estimated annual pension income.

5. Tuition (full-time and part-time) – Fill in this section if you are a student at a university or college, or an educational institution certified by Employment and Social Development Canada, and you will pay more than $100 per institution in tuition fees. Enter the total tuition fees that you will pay if you are a full-time or part-time student.

6. Disability amount – If you will claim the disability amount on your income tax and benefit return by using Form T2201, Disability Tax Credit Certificate, enter $9,872.

7. Spouse or common-law partner amount – Enter the difference between the amount on line 1 (line 1 plus $2,616 if your spouse or common-law partner is **infirm**) and your spouse's or common-law partner's estimated net income for the year if **two** of the following conditions apply:

* You are supporting your spouse or common-law partner who lives with you

* Your spouse or common-law partner's net income for the year will be less than the amount on line 1 (line 1 plus $2,616 if your spouse or common-law partner is **infirm**)

In all cases, go to line 9 if your spouse or common-law partner is **infirm** and has a net income for the year of $28,041 or less.

8. Amount for an eligible dependant – Enter the difference between the amount on line 1 (line 1 plus $2,616 if your eligible dependant is **infirm**) and your eligible dependant's estimated net income for the year if **all** of the following conditions apply:

* You do **not** have a spouse or common-law partner, or you **have** a spouse or common-law partner who does not live with you and who you are not supporting or being supported by

* You are supporting the dependant who is related to you and lives with you

* The dependant's net income for the year will be less than the amount on line 1 (line 1 plus $2,616 if your dependant is **infirm** and you **cannot** claim the Canada caregiver amount for infirm children under 18 years of age for this dependant)

In all cases, go to line 9 if your dependant is **18 years or older**, **infirm**, and has a net income for the year of $28,041 or less.

9. Canada caregiver amount for eligible dependant or spouse or common-law partner – Fill out this section if, at any time in the year, you support an **infirm** eligible dependant (aged 18 or older) **or** an **infirm** spouse or common-law partner whose net income for the year will be $28,041 or less. To calculate the amount you may enter here, fill out the line 9 section of Form TD1-WS.

10. Canada caregiver amount for dependant(s) age 18 or older – If, at any time in the year, you support an **infirm** dependant age 18 or older (**other than** the spouse or common-law partner or eligible dependant you claimed an amount for on line 9 or could have claimed an amount for if their net income were under $15,705) whose net income for the year will be $19,666 or less, enter $8,375. You may enter a partial amount if their net income for the year will be between $19,666 and $28,041. To calculate a partial amount, fill out the line 10 section of Form TD1-WS. This worksheet may also be used to calculate your part of the amount if you are sharing it with another caregiver who supports the same dependant. You may claim this amount for more than one infirm dependant age 18 or older.

11. Amounts transferred from your spouse or common-law partner – If your spouse or common-law partner will not use all of their age amount, pension income amount, tuition amount, or disability amount on their income tax and benefit return, enter the unused amount.

12. Amounts transferred from a dependant – If your dependant will not use all of their disability amount on their income tax and benefit return, enter the unused amount. If your or your spouse's or common-law partner's dependent child or grandchild will not use all of their tuition amount on their income tax and benefit return, enter the unused amount.

13. TOTAL CLAIM AMOUNT – Add lines 1 to 12.
Your employer or payer will use this amount to determine the amount of your tax deductions.

TD1 E (24)   (Ce formulaire est disponible en français.)   Page 1 of 2   Canadä

~ 26 ~

Filling out Form TD1

Fill out this form **only** if any of the following apply:

- you have a new employer or payer, and you will receive salary, wages, commissions, pensions, employment insurance benefits, or any other remuneration
- you want to change the amounts you previously claimed (for example, the number of your eligible dependants has changed)
- you want to claim the deduction for living in a prescribed zone
- you want to increase the amount of tax deducted at source

Sign and date it, and give it to your employer or payer.

More than one employer or payer at the same time

☐ If you have more than one employer or payer at the same time and you have already claimed personal tax credit amounts on another Form TD1 for 2024, you **cannot** claim them again. If your total income from all sources will be more than the personal tax credits you claimed on another Form TD1, check this box, enter "0" on Line 13 and do not fill in Lines 2 to 12.

Total income is less than the total claim amount

☐ Tick this box if your total income for the year from **all** employers and payers will be **less** than your total claim amount on line 13. Your employer or payer will not deduct tax from your earnings.

For non-resident only (Tick the box that applies to you.)

As a non-resident, will 90% or more of your world income be included in determining your taxable income earned in Canada in 2024?

☐ Yes (Fill out the previous page.)

☐ No (Enter "0" on line 13, and do not fill in lines 2 to 12 as you are not entitled to the personal tax credits.)

Call the international tax and non-resident enquiries line at **1-800-959-8281** if you are unsure of your residency status.

Provincial or territorial personal tax credits return

You also have to fill out a provincial or territorial TD1 form if your claim amount on line 13 is more than $15,000. Use the Form TD1 for your province or territory of **employment** if you are an employee. Use the Form TD1 for your province or territory of **residence** if you are a pensioner. Your employer or payer will use both this federal form and your most recent provincial or territorial Form TD1 to determine the amount of your tax deductions.

Your employer or payer will deduct provincial or territorial taxes after allowing the provincial or territorial basic personal amount if you are claiming the basic personal amount **only**.

> **Note:** You may be able to claim the child amount on Form TD1SK, 2024 Saskatchewan Personal Tax Credits Return if you are a Saskatchewan resident supporting children under 18 at any time during 2024. Therefore, you may want to fill out Form TD1SK even if you are **only** claiming the basic personal amount on this form.

Deduction for living in a prescribed zone

You may claim **any** of the following amounts if you live in the Northwest Territories, Nunavut, Yukon, or another prescribed **northern** zone for more than six months in a row beginning or ending in 2024:

- $11.00 for each day that you live in the prescribed northern zone
- $22.00 for each day that you live in the prescribed northern zone if, during that time, you live in a dwelling that you maintain, and you are the only person living in that dwelling who is claiming this deduction

Employees living in a prescribed **intermediate** zone may claim 50% of the total of the above amounts.
For more information, go to **canada.ca/taxes-northern-residents**.

$ _____

Additional tax to be deducted

You may want to have more tax deducted from each payment if you receive other income such as non-employment income from CPP or QPP benefits, or old age security pension. You may have less tax to pay when you file your income tax and benefit return by doing this. Enter the additional tax amount you want deducted from each payment to choose this option. You may fill out a new Form TD1 to change this deduction later.

$ _____

Reduction in tax deductions

You may ask to have less tax deducted at source if you are eligible for deductions or non-refundable tax credits that are not listed on this form (for example, periodic contributions to a registered retirement savings plan (RRSP), child care or employment expenses, charitable donations, and tuition and education amounts carried forward from the previous year). To make this request, fill out Form T1213, Request to Reduce Tax Deductions at Source, to get a letter of authority from your tax services office. Give the letter of authority to your employer or payer. You do not need a letter of authority if your employer deducts RRSP contributions from your salary.

Forms and publications

To get our forms and publications, go to **canada.ca/cra-forms-publications** or call **1-800-959-5525**.

Certification

I certify that the information given on this form is correct and complete.

Signature _____

Date _____

It is a serious offence to make a false return.

Fundamental Canadian Payroll Administration

Pay Statement Guidelines:

Reference: National Payroll Institute (NPI)

Pay Statement Legislative Requirements:

Reference: National Payroll Institute (NPI)

https://payroll.ca/getmedia/ed1d5fd9-32d4-4639-9e6f-88a85e5c3bb4/NPI-Pay-Statement-Guidelines-ENG.pdf

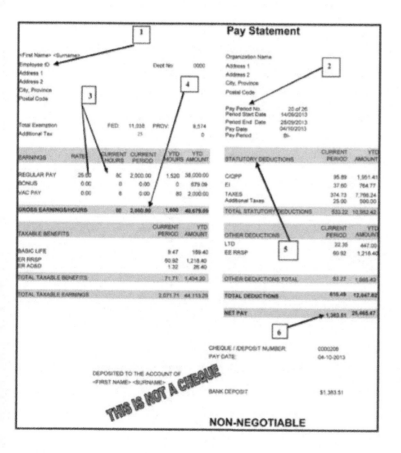

1 Employee information
2 Pay period information
3 Rate and hours information
4 Gross earnings
5 Statutory deductions
6 Net pay

PAY STATEMENT LEGISLATIVE REQUIREMENTS

Legislative requirements and/or CPA recommended:	Canada Labour Code, Part III	Alberta	British Columbia	Manitoba	New Brunswick	Newfoundland and Labrador	Northwest Territories	Nova Scotia	Nunavut	Ontario	Prince Edward Island	Quebec	Saskatchewan	Yukon
Employee Name	*	*	*	*	*	*	*	*	*	*	✔	✔	✔	*
Employer Name	*	*	✔	*	*	*	*	*	*	*	✔	✔	*	*
Pay Period Date	✔	✔	*	*	✔	✔	✔	✔	✔	✔	✔	✔	✔	✔
Date of Payment	*	*	*	*	*	*	*	*	*	*	*	✔	*	*
Rate	✔	✔	✔	✔	*	✔	✔	✔	✔	✔	✔	✔	✔	✔
Hours (Total hours worked/banked)	✔	✔	✔	✔	*	✔	✔	✔	✔	*	✔	✔	✔	✔
Gross Earnings	*	*	✔	✔	✔	✔	*	*	*	✔	✔	✔	✔	✔
Itemized Deductions	✔	✔	✔	✔	✔	✔	✔	✔	✔	✔	✔	✔	✔	✔
Net Pay	✔	*	✔	✔	✔	✔	✔	✔	✔	✔	✔	✔	✔	✔
Regular Wages	*	✔	*	✔	*	*	*	*	*	*	*	*	*	*
Vacation Pay	*	✔	1	*	*	✔	*	*	*	1|2	✔	✔	✔	*
Statutory/Public/General Holiday Pay/Hours	*	✔	1	*	*	*	✔	*	*	1	1	✔	✔	*
Other Earnings/Payments	*	*	✔	*	*	*	*	*	*	✔	✔	✔	*	*
Bonus	*	*	✔	*	*	*	5	*	5	1	1	✔	*	*
Commissions	*	*	1	*	*	*	*	*	*	1	1	✔	*	*
Allowances (living)	*	*	✔	*	*	*	5	*	5	✔	✔	✔	*	*
Overtime Wages	*	✔	✔	✔	*	*	*	*	*	1	1	✔	*	*
Overtime Banked Time Taken	*	✔	✔	*	*	*	*	*	*	*	*	*	*	*
Overtime Banked Time		✔	✔											
Overtime Rate (1.5x or 2x)		✔	✔			✔				1	1	✔		
Declared/Allocated Tips												✔		
Employer Address			✔									✔		
Occupation												✔		
Changes in Rates/Deduction Amounts				✔										
Electronic Statement	3	3	3	3	3	3	3	3	3	3	3	4	3	3

✔ Legislative Requirements
* NPI recommended minimum

1 Other earnings/payments
2 Vacation pay reporting requirement
3 Employee must have confidential access to view and print

4 Employee must have confidential access to view and print and employee must always be given a paper statement if requested
5 Details of bonus or living allowances must be provided upon employee's request

Remuneration

Remuneration is the total compensation paid to an employee.

It includes a base salary, and any financial benefit the employee receives from the employer. Compensation may include indirect payments of money or taxable fringe benefits.

Remuneration and its components reflect an employee's value to the company.

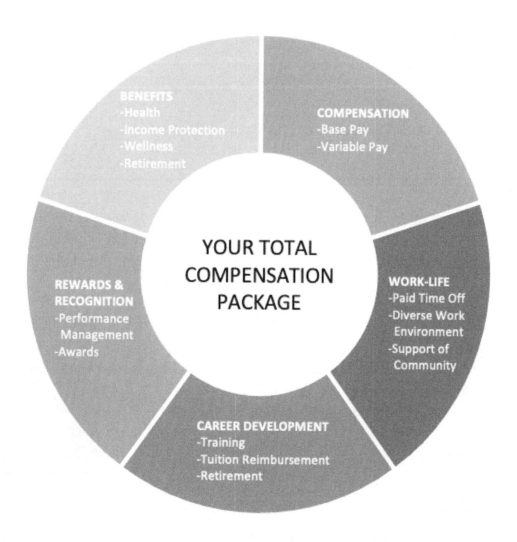

3. EMPLOYMENT INCOME

An individual working for an employer receives compensation or pay for the services they perform. Where an employee-employer relationship exists, this is referred to as employment income.

- Salary
- Hourly
- Piece rate
- Disability pays
- Vacation pays
- Overtime premium
- Shift premium

Allowances

Allowances are additional dollar amounts paid to employees for use, or anticipated use, of their personal property for business purposes. These are fixed amounts that a company gives its employees up front to cover the expenses of certain items.

Common types of allowances include

- Car
- Meals
- Uniforms
- Safety shoes
- Specialized clothing

Expense Reimbursement

Expense reimbursements are dollar amounts paid to employees to cover expenses they incur while performing their job. This is NOT considered employment income.

Hours of Work in BC

When it comes to getting paid for time worked, both employers and employees should have a shared basic understanding.

Standard Hours

- Standard is 8 hours per day, or 40 hours per week

Overtime Hours

- Overtime is more than 8 hours per day, or more than 40 hours per week, in BC
  - Rate of pay increases by 1.5 times the standard rate
- Double time is time worked more than 12 hours in a day in BC
  - Rate of pay increased by 2.0 times the standard rate

Banked Overtime

- Part or all can be paid out
- Used at a future date as agreed upon by the employer and the employee
- Employer to pay out banked overtime if employee provides one month's written notice

Extra Pay for Working During the Rest Period

- Paid at a rate of time and a half
- Can be paid for the day with the least hours (i.e., works 7 days in a row, even if less than 8 hours or less than 40 hours per week)

Meal and Coffee Breaks

- Employer not required to provide coffee breaks
- If working more than 5 hours, the employee is required to have, at minimum, a 30-minute unpaid meal break. Note that if the employee is required to work or be available to work, then the meal break becomes a paid meal break.

Split Shift

- The workday is the combined total of hours worked within a 12-hour period (ex. if an employee has a split shift with a start time of 8am, the shift must be completed by 8pm that day)

Travel to Work

- Can be paid at a different rate, but not less than minimum wage
- Not considered work hours even if driving a company provided vehicle, or employee is picked up by the employer or another employee
- It is considered work if the employee is providing service to the employer (ex. bringing the employer's provided tools, or equipment to the worksite)
- If the employee is asked by the employer to pick up other employees and bring them to the worksite

BC Employment Standards Video: Hours of Work and Overtime in BC

https://www.youtube.com/watch?v=Yw5BQJkXApk

SHIFT PREMIUMS

Additional amounts paid over and above an employee's normal salary or hourly rate for working on an evening or midnight shift.

A fixed dollar amount per hour worked on the shift:

Shift premium = Fixed dollar amount x Hours worked on shift

Example:

Tamara works for XYZ Corp in BC, with a biweekly pay cycle. Tamara is paid $18 per hour; she is entitled to OT pay; She works afternoon shifts which has a premium of .50 cents per hour. (6 points). Calculate her pay.

Day	Mon	Tue	Wed	Thu	Fri	Sat	Sun	Total
Week 1	8	10	6	8	8			40
Week 2	8	8	8	8	8	6		46

Total Regular Hours:	78
Total Overtime hours:	8
Total Regular Pay	$1,404.00
Total Overtime Pay	$216.00
Total Premium Pay	$43.00
Total Gross Pay	$1,663.00

PIECEWORK

The rate of pay earned per unit of production, regardless of the time to complete.

Regular earnings = Rate x Number of pieces

BONUS

Non-Discretionary

- Performance based, profit sharing plan
- Vacationable earnings

Discretionary

- Pre-employment, referral, retention, or celebratory event
- Non Vacationable earnings

Special Payments

Retroactive pay

Profit Sharing

Retiring Allowance

Special Payment Chart

Reference:

https://www.canada.ca/en/revenue-agency/services/tax/businesses/topics/payroll/payroll-deductions-contributions/special-payments/special-payments-chart.html

Fundamental Canadian Payroll Administration

Special payments chart - Canada.ca

List of special payments and their respective deductions (CPP, EI and tax)

Special payments	CPP contributions [Note 1]	EI premiums [Note 1]	Tax deductions
Advances	Yes	Yes	Yes
Benefits under the Employment Insurance Act	No	No	Yes
Bonuses and retroactive pay increases or irregular amounts	Yes	Yes	Yes
Casual employment if it is for a purpose other than your usual trade or business (even if there is a contract of employment)	No	No	No
Caregiving benefits – amounts paid to cover the waiting period or to increase the benefit	Yes	Yes/No (Note 2)	Yes
Corporate employee who controls more than 40% of the corporation's voting shares receiving salary, wages or other remuneration	Yes	No	Yes
Directors' fees paid to residents of Canada or non-residents – Fee only	Yes (Note 3)	No	Yes (Note 4)
Directors' fees paid to residents of Canada or non-residents – Fee in addition to salary	Yes/No (Note 5)	Yes/No (Note 5)	Yes
Employees profit sharing plan (EPSP)	No	No	No
Employment in Canada by a foreign government or an international organization	Yes/No (Note 6)	Yes/No (Note 7)	Yes (Note 8)
Employment in Canada of a non-resident person if the unemployment insurance laws of any foreign country require someone to pay premiums for that employment	Yes/No (Note 9)	No	Yes (Note 8)
Employment in Canada under an exchange program if the employer paying the remuneration is not resident in Canada	Yes/No (Note 10)	No	Yes (Note 8)

Employment of your child or a person that you maintain if no cash remuneration is paid	No	No	No
Employment that is an exchange of work or service (even if there is a contract of service)	Yes/No (Note 11)	No	Yes/No (Note 12)
Employment under the "Self-employment assistance" or "Job creation partnerships" benefit program established under section 59 of the Employment Insurance Act, or under a similar benefit program that a provincial government or other organization provides and is part of an agreement under section 63 of the Employment Insurance Act.	Yes/No (Note 13)	No	Yes/No (Note 14)
Employment when employment insurance premiums have to be paid according to the unemployment insurance laws of any state of the United States, the District of Columbia, Puerto Rico, or the Virgin Islands, or according to the Railroad Unemployment Insurance Act of the United States	Yes/No (Note 10)	No	Yes
Entertainment activity, employment in	Yes	Yes	Yes
Furlough, amounts received when on	Yes	Yes	Yes
Honorariums from employment or office	Yes/No (Note 15)	Yes/No (Note 15)	Yes
Incentive payments	Yes	Yes	Yes
Job creation Employment and Social Development Canada approved project, additional amounts that you as an employer pay while participating in a project	Yes/No (Note 16)	No	Yes
Lost-time pay from a union, amounts received as	Yes	Yes	Yes
Maternity benefits – amounts paid to cover the waiting period or to increase the benefit	Yes	Yes/No (Note 2)	Yes
Overtime pay, including banked overtime pay	Yes	Yes	Yes
Parental care benefits – amounts paid to cover the waiting period or to increase the benefit	Yes	Yes/No (Note 2)	Yes

Payments to placement and employment agency workers – Agency that hires employees	Yes	Yes	Yes
Payments to placement and employment agency workers – Agency pays the worker	Yes	Yes	No
Payments to placement and employment agency workers – Client of the agency pays the worker	Yes	No	Yes
Payments to placement and employment agency workers – Agency hires a self-employed worker	No	No	No
Payments under Part 2 of the Veterans' Well being Act – amounts received on account of an earnings loss benefit, supplementary retirement benefit or permanent impairment allowance payable to the taxpayer	No	No	Yes
Qualifying retroactive lump-sum payments (Note 17)	Yes	Yes	Yes
Retirement compensation arrangements (RCA)	No	No	Yes
Retiring allowances (also called severance pay)	No	No	Yes (Note 18)
Sabbatical, remuneration received while on	Yes	Yes	Yes
Salary	Yes	Yes	Yes
Salary deferral – non-prescribed plans or arrangements – on amounts earned	Yes	Yes	Yes
Salary deferral – prescribed plans or arrangements – on amounts received	Yes/No (Note 19)	Yes/No (Note 19)	Yes
Sick leave, amounts received while on sick leave, sick leave credits, payments for	Yes	Yes	Yes
Spouse or common-law partner, employment of, if you cannot deduct the remuneration paid as an expense under the Income Tax Act	No	Yes/No (Note 20)	Yes

Teacher on exchange from a foreign country, employment of	No	Yes/No (Note 21)	Yes/No (Note 22)
Tips and gratuities (controlled by employer)	Yes	Yes	Yes (Note 23)
Tips and gratuities (direct tips or gratuities – not controlled by the employer)	No	No	No (Note 23)
Vacation pay and public holidays, and lump-sum vacation payment	Yes	Yes	Yes (Note 16)
Vow of poverty – employment of a member of a religious order who has taken a vow of poverty. This applies whether the remuneration is paid directly to the order or the member pays it to the order.	No	No	Yes/No (Note 24)
Wages	Yes	Yes	Yes
Wages in lieu of termination notice	Yes	Yes	Yes
Wage-loss replacement plans – Paid by the employer	Yes	Yes	Yes
Wage-loss replacement plans – Paid by third party/trustee and the employer: • funds any part of the plan • exercises a degree of control over the plan • directly or indirectly determines the eligibility for benefits	Yes	Yes	Yes
Workers' compensation claims – Employee's salary paid before or after a workers' compensation board claim is decided	Yes	Yes	Yes
Workers' compensation claims – Advances or loans equal to the workers' compensation benefits awarded	No	No	No
Workers' compensation claims – Amount paid in addition to an advance or loan before the claim is accepted	Yes	Yes (Note 25)	Yes

Fundamental Canadian Payroll Administration

Workers' compensation claims – Top-up amounts paid after the claim is accepted	Yes	No	Yes
Workers' compensation claims – Top-up amounts paid as sick leave after the claim is accepted	Yes	No	Yes

Note 1 If you have already deducted the total yearly maximum contributions from the employee's income, do not deduct more contributions. Do not consider amounts deducted by previous employers during the same year unless there was a restructure or reorganization.

Note 2 Do not deduct EI premiums if the following two conditions are met:

- the total amount of your payment and the EI weekly benefits combined do not exceed the employee's normal weekly gross salary
- your payment does not reduce any other accumulated employment benefits such as banked sick leave, vacation leave credits, or retiring allowance

Note 3 Do not deduct CPP contributions when the employment is performed totally or partly outside Canada.

Note 4 Do not deduct income tax if you estimate that the total fee paid in the year is less than the total claim amount on Form TD1.

Note 5 The issue of whether to deduct CPP, EI or both depends on the status of the resident director's employment. See Directors' fees.

Note 6 Deduct CPP contributions when the international organization or the foreign government agrees to cover their employees. A list of the international organizations and foreign countries can be found under schedules [V] and [VII] of the Canada Pension Plan Regulations (except for employment listed in schedules [VI] and VIII).

Note 7 Deduct EI premiums when the foreign government or international organization agrees to cover its Canadian employees under Canada's EI legislation (in this case, the employment is insurable if Employment and Social Development Canada agrees).

Note 8 For more information on non-resident employees, see Rendering services in Canada.

Note 9 Deduct CPP contributions unless the worker has a certificate of coverage from the competent authority of their country confirming that the worker is contributing to a pension plan in their country. Do not deduct CPP contributions if the employer is not residing in Canada and does not have an establishment in Canada, unless the employer has filed a Form CPT13, Application for an Employer Resident Outside Canada to Cover Employment in Canada Under the Canada Pension.

Note 10 Do not deduct CPP contributions unless the employer has filed a Form CPT13, Application for an Employer Resident Outside Canada to Cover Employment in Canada Under the Canada Pension.

Note 11 Deduct CPP contributions, unless the employment does not require CPP deductions, as indicated in Chapter 2 of Guide T4001, Employers' Guide – Payroll Deductions and Remittances.

Note 12 For more information about bartering, see archived Interpretation Bulletin IT-490, Barter Transactions. Do not deduct income tax unless the taxpayer is an employee and makes a regular habit of providing services for cash.

Note 13 Do not deduct CPP contributions on benefits paid by Employment and Social Development Canada or a provincial government. Deduct CPP contributions on payments made by an employer unless the individual is working as a self-employed individual or the employment does not require CPP contributions, as indicated in Chapter 2 of Guide T4001, Employers' Guide – Payroll Deductions and Remittances.

Note 14 Deduct income tax if the payment is considered government financial assistance. But if the payment is considered an inducement to earn business income, do not deduct income tax.

Note 15 To determine if you have to deduct CPP, EI, or both for individuals who hold an office, see Elected or appointed officials.

Note 16 Deduct CPP contributions on payments made by an employer unless the individual is working as a self-employed individual or the employment does not require CPP contributions, as indicated in Chapter 2 of Guide T4001, Employers' Guide – Payroll Deductions and Remittances.

Note 17 To determine if you have to deduct CPP, EI or both, see Prescribed salary deferral plans or arrangements.

Note 18 Qualifying retroactive lump-sum payments may require CPP or EI deductions in addition to income tax.

Note 19 Do not deduct income tax on the amount of retiring allowance that is transferred directly to the recipient's RPP or RRSP (up to the amount of the employee's available RRSP deduction limit). See Retiring allowances for details.

Note 20 Deduct EI premiums if you would have negotiated a similar contract with a person that you deal with at arm's length.

Note 21 Deduct EI premiums, unless the worker is remunerated by an employer residing outside Canada.

Note 22 You have to deduct income tax on Canadian earnings, unless provisions of an income tax convention or treaty say otherwise.

Did the employer give the employee a benefit or an allowance or an expense reimbursement?

Benefit:

- The employee has received a benefit that the employer paid or gave something that benefits the employee.
- A benefit is a good or service the employer gives or arranges for a third party to give to your employee, such as free use of property that you own.
- A benefit includes an allowance or a reimbursement of an employee's personal expense.

Allowance

- An allowance or an advance is any periodic or lump-sum amount that you pay to your employee on top of salary or wages, to help the employee pay for certain anticipated expenses without having them support the expenses.

- An allowance or advance is a subjective amount, for a specific purpose and receipts are not required.

Reimbursement

- An amount you pay to your employee to repay expenses he or she had while carrying out the duties of employment. The employee has to keep proper records (detailed receipts) to support the expenses and give them to you.

*Reference: CRA

Statutory Holiday Pay in BC

To qualify for statutory holiday pay, an employee must be employed for 30 calendar days and have worked 15 of the 30 days before a statutory holiday.

Statutory Holiday Pay

Total wages ÷ number of days worked = statutory holiday pay

*Total wages – salary, commission, vacation (Don't include overtime)

*Days worked during the 30 calendar days before the statutory holiday

*Usually, an average days' pay

Exclusions may include managers, IT professionals, commission sales, nursing, emergency responders and union agreements.

Holiday	Date in 2024	Observance
New Year's Day	January 1, Monday	National
Islander Day	February 19, Monday	PEI
Louis Riel Day	February 19, Monday	MB
Heritage Day	February 19, Monday	NS
Family Day	February 19, Monday	BC, AB, SK, ON, NB
Valentine's Day	February 14, Wednesday	Not an official holiday
Leap Day	February 29, Thursday	Not a holiday
St. Patrick's Day	March 17, Sunday	Not a stat holiday
Good Friday	March 29, Friday	National except QC
Easter Monday	April 1, Monday	QC
Mother's Day	May 12, Sunday	Not an official holiday
Victoria Day	May 20, Monday	National except NS, NL
Father's Day	June 16, Sunday	Not an official holiday
Aboriginal Day	June 21, Friday	NWT
St. Jean Baptiste Day	June 24, Monday	QC
Canada Day	July 1, Monday	National
Civic Holiday	August 5, Monday	AB, BC, SK, ON, MB, NB, NU
Labour Day	September 2, Monday	National
National Day for Truth and Reconciliation	September 30, Monday	National, federally regulated workplaces only
Thanksgiving	October 14, Monday	National except NS, NL
Halloween	October 31, Thursday	Not an official holiday
Remembrance Day	November 11, Monday	National except MB, ON, QC, NS
Christmas Day	December 25, Wednesday	National
Boxing Day	December 26, Thursday	ON

Gross to Net Steps

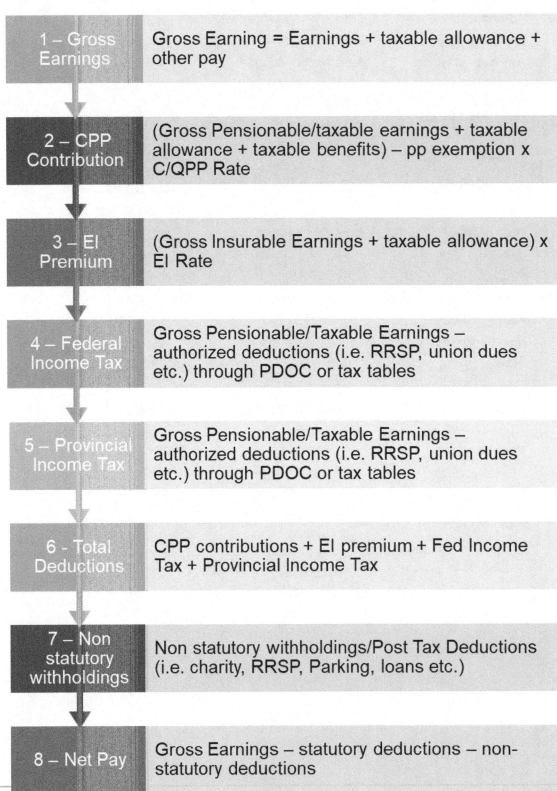

1 – Gross Earnings	Gross Earning = Earnings + taxable allowance + other pay
2 – CPP Contribution	(Gross Pensionable/taxable earnings + taxable allowance + taxable benefits) – pp exemption x C/QPP Rate
3 – EI Premium	(Gross Insurable Earnings + taxable allowance) x EI Rate
4 – Federal Income Tax	Gross Pensionable/Taxable Earnings – authorized deductions (i.e. RRSP, union dues etc.) through PDOC or tax tables
5 – Provincial Income Tax	Gross Pensionable/Taxable Earnings – authorized deductions (i.e. RRSP, union dues etc.) through PDOC or tax tables
6 - Total Deductions	CPP contributions + EI premium + Fed Income Tax + Provincial Income Tax
7 – Non statutory withholdings	Non statutory withholdings/Post Tax Deductions (i.e. charity, RRSP, Parking, loans etc.)
8 – Net Pay	Gross Earnings – statutory deductions – non-statutory deductions

Fundamental Canadian Payroll Administration

4. TIME OFF AND LEAVES

Vacation Pay

Vacation Pay rates and entitlements in Canada

The ESA outlines Vacation Pay. Annual leave must be taken within 12 months of being earned. Employers may schedule vacation time according to the needs of the business.

Vacation Pay - Act Part 7, Section 58 - Province of British Columbia (gov.bc.ca)

Reference:

https://www2.gov.bc.ca/gov/content/employment-business/employment-standards-advice/employment-standards/forms-resources/igm/esa-part-7-section-58

Length of employment Employment	Vacation Time			Vacation Pay Percent
	Weeks	Days		
After 1 year of employment	2	10	OR	4%
After 5 years of employment	3	15	OR	6%
After 10 years of employment	4	20	OR	8%

Annual Leave (Time off) in BC

- Must take time off within 12 months of being earned
- Cannot skip and receive pay
- Vacation days can be taken before it is earned – deduct – written agreement
- At least 4% of all wages paid in the previous year
- After 5 years of employment, 6% of all wages
- When employment ends, employees must receive all vacation accrued

British Columbia

Vacation Pay	4% for the first 5 years
	6% after 5 years
Vacation Entitlements	After 1 year - 2 weeks
	After 5 years - 3 weeks

Alberta

Vacation Pay	4% for the first 4 years
	6% after 5 years
Vacation Entitlements	After 1 year - 2 weeks
	After 5 years - 3 weeks

Saskatchewan

Vacation Pay	3/52 (5.77%) for the first 9 years
	4/52 (7.69%) after 10 years
Vacation Entitlements	After 1 year - 3 weeks
	After 10 years - 4 weeks

Nova Scotia

Vacation Pay	4% for the first 7 years
	6% at the start of the 8th year
Vacation Entitlements	After 12 months - 2 weeks
	After 8 years - 3 weeks

Prince Edward Island

Vacation Pay	4% for less than 8 years
	6% after 8 years
Vacation Entitlements	1 to less than 8 years – 2 weeks
	8 years or more - 3 weeks

Newfoundland & Labrador

Vacation Pay	4% up to 15 years
	6% after 15 years
Vacation Entitlements	1 to 15 years - 2 weeks
	15 years or more - 3 weeks

Yukon

Vacation Pay	4%
Vacation Entitlements	After 1 year - 2 weeks

Reference: National Payroll Institute (NPI)

DETAILED VACATIONABLE EARNINGS

CLC = *Canada Labour Code, Part III*   **Y** = Included   **N** = Not included

Earning type	CLC	BC	AB	SK	MB	ON	QC	NB	PE	NS	NL	YK	NT/NU
Regular salary/earnings													
Regular salary	Y	Y	Y	Y	Y	Y	Y	Y	Y	Y	Y	Y	Y
Call-in pay	Y	Y	Y	Y	Y	Y	Y	Y	Y	Y	Y	Y	Y
Overtime	Y	Y	N	N	Y	Y	Y	Y	Y	Y	Y	Y	Y
Retroactive pay	Y	Y	Y	Y	Y	Y	Y	Y	Y	Y	Y	Y	Y
Shift premium	Y	Y	Y	Y	Y	Y	Y	Y	Y	Y	Y	Y	Y
Standby pay	Y	N	N	Y	N	Y	Y	*	Y	Y	N	N	N
Statutory holiday pay	Y	Y	N	Y	Y	Y	Y	N	Y	Y	Y	Y	Y
Vacation pay (previously paid)	Y	Y	Y	Y	N	N	Y	N	N	N	Y	N	Y
Allowances													
Car	N[7]	N	N	N	N	N	Y[10]	N	N	N	N	N	N
Clothing	N[7]	N	N	N	N	N	Y[10]	N	N	N	N	N	N
Housing	N[7]	N	N	N	N	Y	Y[10]	N	N	N	N	N	N
Meal	N[7]	N	N	N	N	N	Y[10]	N	N	N	N	N	N
Moving	N[7]	N	N	N	N	N	Y[10]	N	N	N	N	N	N
Tool	N[7]	N	N	N	N	N	Y[10]	N	N	N	N	N	N
Travel	N[7]	N	N	N	N	N	Y[10]	N	N	N	N	N	N
Bonuses													
Discretionary	N	N	N	N	N	N	N	N	N	N	N	N	N
Work Related	Y	Y	Y	Y	Y	Y	Y	Y	Y	Y	Y	Y	Y
Commissions													
Earned at employer's premises	Y	Y	Y	Y	Y	Y	Y	Y	Y[8]	Y	Y	Y	Y
Earned away from employer's premises	Y	Y	N	Y	Y	N	Y	Y	Y[8]	N	Y	Y	Y
Earned by a route salesperson	Y	Y	Y	Y	Y	Y	Y	Y	Y[8]	Y	Y	Y	Y
Directors' Fees													
Employee	N	N	N	N	N	N	Y	N[3]	N	N	N	N	*
Non-employee	N	N	N	N	N	N	Y	N[3]	N	N	N	N	*

Earning type	CLC	BC	AB	SK	MB	ON	QC	NB	PE	NS	NL	YK	NT/NU
Miscellaneous earnings													
Maternity leave top-ups	N	N	N	N	N	N	Y[10]	N	N	N	N	N	N
Profit sharing payments	Y[2]	N	N[1]	Y	N[1]	Y[5]	Y	N	N	N	N	N	Y
Tips – employer controlled	N	N	N	N	Y	N	Y	N	N	N	N	N	N
Termination payments													
Retiring Allowance (lump-sum)	N	N	N	N	N	N	N	N	N	N	N	Y[7]	N
Retiring Allowance (installments)	N	N	N	N	N	N	N	N	N	N	N	Y[7]	N
Pay in lieu of notice (as required by Employment Standards)	N*	Y	N	Y	N	Y	Y	Y	Y	Y	N	Y	Y
Salary Continuance	N	N	N	N	N	N	N	N	N	N	N	N	N
Taxable benefits													
Awards/Gifts Kind	N	N	N	N	N	N	Y[10]	N	N	N	N	N	N
Board and Lodging	N	N	Y	Y	Y	Y	Y[10]	N	Y	Y[4]	N	N	N
Company owned/leased vehicle	Y	N	N	N	N	N	Y[10]	N	N	N	N	N	N
Group term life insurance	N	N	N	N	N	N	Y[10]	N	N	N	N	N	N
Group RRSP plan payments	N	N	N	N	N	N	Y[10]	N	N	N	N	N	N
Interest free loans	N	N	N	N	N	N	Y[10]	N	N	N	N	N	N
Parking	N	N	N	N	N	N	Y[10]	N	N	N	N	N	N
Provincial medical	n/a	N	N	n/a	n/a	n/a	n/a	n/a	n/a	n/a	n/a	n/a	n/a
Stock options	N	N	N	N	N	N	Y[10]	N	N	N	N	N	N

Legislative Leaves	CLC	BC	AB	SK	MB	ON	QC	NB	PE	NS	NL	YK	NT/NU
Bereavement Leave	Y	N	N	N	N	N	Y	N	Y	N	Y	N	N
Domestic Violence	N	N	N	N	Y	N	Y	N	N	N	Y	N	N
Jury Duty	N	N	N	N	N	N	N	N	N	N	Y	N	N
Paternity Leave	N	N	N	N	N	N	Y	N	N	N	N	N	N
Personal Emergency Leave	N	N	N	N	N	N	Y	N	N	N	N	N	N
Sick Leave	N	N	N	N	N	N	Y	N	Y	N	N	N	N
Voting Leave	N	N	N	Y	N	Y	Y	N	N	N	N	N	N
Wedding Leave	N	N	N	N	N	N	Y	N	N	N	N	N	N

[1] Unless tied to hours of work, production or efficiency

[2] If included in wages or remuneration for work

[3] Included where fee is a "wage" (condition of employment). Excluded where fee is an honoraria

[4] Determined on a case by case basis

[5] Excluded if part of DPSP

[6] If amount is taxable

[7] Included in unique circumstances

[8] Majority earned must be salary

[9] Housing and meal included if part of employment contract in Ontario

[10] All taxable benefits and allowances in Quebec would be classified as vacationable under certain conditions. Employers should contact Quebec Labour Standards (CNESST) in order to obtain additional information

* = Not clearly addressed in legislation

Fundamental Canadian Payroll Administration

Sick Pay

PAID SICK LEAVE IN BRITISH COLUMBIA

Effective January 1, 2022, workers in B.C. will be entitled to permanent paid sick leave comes into effect with **5 paid sick days each year**. Both full- and part-time employees are eligible for this benefit.

Prior to January 1, 2022, illness and injury leave was unavailable to many employees in B.C. On January 1, 2022, changes to the Employments Standards Act RSBC 1998 c. 113 (ESA) were implemented with the result that full-time, part-time, temporary and casual employees in B.C are now entitled to illness and injury leave pursuant to Part 6 of the ESA, unless they are excluded by regulation.

Employees excluded under the ESA include employees in federally regulated sectors who are entitled to sick leave pursuant to Part III of the Canada Labour Code RSC 1985 c. L-2 (10 days paid illness and injury leave) ; independent contractors and self-employed workers and employees in professions and occupations listed in sections 31 and 32 of the ESA. These include, but are not limited to, lawyers, dentists, doctors, architects, and accountants.

Eligibility

Pursuant to Part 7.02 s. 45.031 of the ESA an employee is entitled **to 5 days of paid leave and 3 days of unpaid leave** for illness and injury per calendar year after they have been employed for 90 days. If the leave is not used within the calendar year, the unused days cannot be carried forward into the following calendar year.

For unexpected illness or life situations an employee is not required to give advance notice, but they are expected to advise their employer as soon as possible if they cannot work due to illness or injury. An employer is allowed to request the employee provide reasonably sufficient proof of the illness or injury.

Leave does not have to be on consecutive days.

Employer responsibilities

Employees must be paid an "average days' pay". The number of hours an employee was scheduled to work on the day they took illness and injury leave is not relevant to the wages owed. Average wage is based on the wages and days worked in the 30 calendar days before the first day the employee went on illness and injury leave. It is calculated as follows:

Total wages ÷ number of days worked = average day's pay

Total wages include regular wages, commissions, statutory holiday pay, annual vacation pay, and sick pay required by this Act, but does not include overtime pay or benefits.

Days worked refers to any days when wages were earned and includes paid annual vacation, paid statutory holidays, or paid sick days.

- The employer is responsible for bearing the cost of illness and injury leave.
- An employer cannot terminate an employee or change any of the conditions of the employee's employment without the employee's written consent as a result of a illness or injury leave or they may be subject to penalties.
- Keep record of Absences
- An employer may send an employee home after they have reported to work if they are unfit for work due to illness or injury, in which case illness or injury leave applies.
- If an employee asks to leave early or is sent home early for illness or injury, they are only paid for time worked or the minimum daily pay (2 hours for shifts less than 8 hours or 4 hours for shifts of 8 or more hours)
- Additional leave is classified as a leave of absence and an ROE may need to be provided to the client so they can obtain Medical EI, or short/long term disability benefits.

References

- https://www2.gov.bc.ca/gov/content/employment-business/employment-standards-advice/paid-sick-leave
- https://www.bclaws.gov.bc.ca/civix/document/id/complete/statreg/396_95#section31
- https://www2.gov.bc.ca/gov/content/employment-business/employment-standards-advice/employment-standards/forms-resources/igm/esa-part-6-section-52-12
- https://www.cfib-fcei.ca/en/tools-resources/employment-standards/bc-sick-days-what-you-need-know
- https://www2.gov.bc.ca/gov/content/employment-business/employment-standards-advice/employment-standards/forms-resources/igm/esa-part-6-section-49-1#:~:text=An%20average%20day's%20pay%20is,during%20that%2030%2Dday%20period

There are several types of "unpaid" leave.

- Maternity and Parental Leave
- Family Responsibility Leave
- Compassionate Care Leave
- Jury Duty Leave
- Bereavement Leave
- Reservist Leave
- Critical Illness or Injury Leave
- Leave Respecting Domestic or Sexual Violence
- Leave Respecting the Disappearance of Child

When leave ends, an employee can come back to their job or one like it. The employer must contact the employee to arrange the employee's return to work.

- An employer cannot terminate (fire or lay off) an employee or change their job conditions without the employee's written agreement.
- If the job no longer exists and there is no similar job, the employee who is ready to return can be terminated but must be given compensation for length of service based on the last day of employment

Reference:

https://www2.gov.bc.ca/gov/content/employment-business/employment-standards-advice/employment-standards/time-off/leaves-of-absence

https://www2.gov.bc.ca/gov/content/employment-business/employment-standards-advice/employment-standards/termination

Types of Leave of Absence in BC

Pregnancy/Maternity	17 weeks of unpaid leave and an additional 6 weeks if unable to return due to delivery
Parental Leave	Up to 62 weeks, 78 weeks (18 months) if combined with pregnancy/maternity leave (17 weeks) plus 61 weeks of unpaid parental leave
Family Responsibility Leave	Up to 5 days per year to attend to health care for an immediate family member under the age of 19 years
Compassionate Care Leave	Up to 27 weeks to care for a gravely ill family member
Bereavement Leave	• Up to 3 days for the death of a member of an employee's immediate family • Does not have to be consecutive days. • Does not have to be for attending a funeral. • Does not have to start on the date of death
Leave Respecting the Disappearance of Child	• 52 weeks if their child disappears because of crime. • Leave ends 14 days after the child is found alive. • The leave also ends if it is probable that the child's disappearance was not the result of a crime or if the employee is charged with a crime in relation to the child's disappearance
Leave Respecting the Death of a Child	• 104 weeks of leave if their child dies. • The leave also ends if the employee is charged with a crime in relation to the child's death

Maternity and Parental Leave in BC

What is it?

Maternity leave and parental leave are statutory rights granted to employees to take unpaid time off from work when they have a baby or adopt a child. The period can go up to 17 weeks of maternity leave and 61 or 62 weeks of parental leave plus any additional leave the employee is entitled under the act that regulates these leaves.

Who can take it?

The maternity leave can be taken by pregnant employees, and it goes up to 17 consecutive weeks. Employees who decide the termination of their pregnancies are entitled to up to 6 consecutive weeks of leave. The period of leave can be extended up to 6 additional consecutive weeks if, for reasons related to the birth or termination of the pregnancy, the employee is unable to return to work.

Paternal leave can be taken by employees who have been parents of a newborn or adopting parents and the period goes up to 61 consecutive weeks for the moms. Dads and adopting parents can take up to 62 consecutive weeks of leave. Parental care period can be extended by up to 5 consecutive weeks when the child has a physical, psychological, or emotional condition.

When can employees take it?

Maternity leave can be taken no earlier than 13 weeks before the expected birth date and no later than they day of birth. Employees who decide the termination of their pregnancies can begin their leave on the date of the termination of the pregnancy. When an extension of leave takes place, it has to be taken consecutively after the regular period of maternity leave.

Paternal leave must begin immediately after the end of the maternity leave for the mom, unless the employee and employer agree otherwise. The leave for dads must begin 78 weeks after the birth of the child and adopting parents have the same period of time as biological fathers but it will count from the day the child is placed with the adopting parents. When an extension of leave takes place, it has to be taken consecutively after the end of the paternal leave.

How do employees take it?

To be able to take maternity leave and parental leave the employee must give a writing request to the employer. The request must be given to the employer at least 4 weeks before the day the employee wants to begin the leave. Employees should give a certificate stating the expected or actual birthday or the date the pregnancy terminated, or other evidence of the employee's entitlement to leave, if it is required by the employer.

Employer responsibilities

Employers may grant maternal and parental leave for the employee. Under this condition the employer cannot:

- Terminate an employee because of their leave and it includes giving a notice of termination immediately upon they return to work after the leave.
- Change a condition of employment without the employee's written consent.

They employer must:

- Place employees in the position they were in before taking the leave or in a comparable position.
- Comply with the employee's placement who returns from leave as soon as operations resume when, due to company needs, operations have been suspended or discontinued at the time of the employee's return.

Reference:

Leaves of absence - Province of British Columbia (gov.bc.ca)

Maternity Leave - Act Part 6, Section 50 - Province of British Columbia (gov.bc.ca)

Parental Leave - Act Part 6, Section 51 - Province of British Columbia (gov.bc.ca)

Duties of Employer - Act Part 6, Section 54 - Province of British Columbia (gov.bc.ca)

Family Responsibility Leave in BC

What

Family Responsibility Leave is a statutory right that is initiated by the employee. It is unpaid leave for up to 5 days in an employee's employment year, based on their start date. It is intended to help employees handle family issues which may conflict with job responsibilities and does not carry over year to year if unused during the year. It must be related to the care or health, and in the case of a child, education, of a member of the employee's immediate family.

Who

The employee is entitled to this leave in order to care for their immediate family which includes the spouse, child, parent, guardian, sibling, grandchild or grandparent of an employee, and any person who lives with an employee as a member of the employee's family. It includes common-law spouses, step-parents, and step-children, and same sex partners and their children as long as they live with the employee as a member of the employee's family.

When

Employees are entitled to request up to 5 days off, to be taken at their discretion. Unless a different agreement has been made, any time taken off on any day (even one hour) qualifies as one day.

How

There is no request process set out in the act, however employees are expected to give the employer reasonable notice of any request for leave to allow the employer to accommodate the absence. The request does not need to be made because of a crisis or emergency.

Employer responsibility

Employers should record the absence as leave without pay and keep a record of the absence. They are also entitled to request proof, after the event, that the request for a leave was valid.

Reference:

- https://www2.gov.bc.ca/gov/content/employment-business/employment-standards-advice/employment-standards/forms-resources/igm/esa-part-6-section-52
- https://www.go2hr.ca/legal/employment-standards-act/family-responsibility-leave#:~:text=While%20there%20is%20no%20request,is%20entitled%20to%20the%20leave.

Compassionate Care Leave in BC

All employees are entitled to 27 weeks of unpaid Compassionate Care Leave, within a 52-week time frame. There is no minimum duration of employment or hours worked to qualify to take this leave. Employers are not allowed to negotiate or deny this leave to an employee if the person they are requesting to take the leave for is an immediate family member or an individual included in the Family Member Regulation list.

Compassionate Leave is available for employees who have a family member or close relative with a serious health condition who has been given the prognosis of a high chance of passing away within 26 weeks. This includes any member of the employee's immediate family, or someone who may not be blood related but is living with the employee as part of the employee's family/household. The definition of "family" can also extend to any individual who is like a close relative to the employee. There is a long list within the interpretation of the Compassionate Care Leave policy, which outlines all the classification of individuals outside of immediate family that would qualify an employee to take this leave.

An employee does not need to give any notice prior to taking the leave, but they do need to provide a certificate of the prognosis from a physician or nurse practitioner as soon as possible. The first day the employee is absent will be the date the leave starts, not from when the medical certificate is provided. The 27 weeks do not have to be taken consecutively. If an employee only takes a few days off during a week, this time is still counted as 1 full week. If the family member does not pass away within the 52 weeks, but the employee has already taken their 27 weeks Compassionate Leave, the employer does not have to grant them an additional 27 weeks until the subsequent 52-week period starts, at which time a new medical certificate will need to be provided.

During an employee's Compassionate Care Leave, their condition of employment cannot be altered without the employee's written consent, and their employment cannot be terminated.

This information is outlined on the Government of BC website, under Compassionate Care Leave-Act Part 6 Section 52.1

5. BENEFITS AND ALLOWANCES

Pensionable Earning vs Non-Pensionable Earnings

Insurable Earnings vs Non-Insurable Earnings

Taxable vs Non-Taxable Benefits

Benefits are dollar values attributed to something the employer has either provided to an employee or paid for on an employee's behalf.

Whether a benefit is taxable depends on the employee or receiving an <u>economic advantage</u> that can be measured in money, and if the individual is the <u>primary beneficiary</u> of the benefit.

Payroll Administrator is responsible for:

- **Determine if the benefit is taxable**
- **Calculate the value of the benefit**
- **Calculate payroll deductions**
- **File an information return**

Employers' Guide – <u>Taxable Benefits and Allowances</u>: Canada Revenue Agency

*Reference:

https://www.canada.ca/en/revenue-agency/services/tax/businesses/topics/payroll/benefits-allowances.html

https://www.canada.ca/en/revenue-agency/services/forms-publications/publications/t4130.html

Taxable allowance or benefit	Deduct CPP[1]	Deduct EI	Code for T4 slip
Automobile and motor vehicle allowances – in cash	yes	yes	40
Automobile standby charge and operating expense benefits – non-cash	yes	no	34
Board and lodging, if **cash** earnings also paid	yes	[2]	30
Cellular phone and Internet services – in cash	yes	yes	40
Cellular phone and Internet services – non-cash	yes	no	40
Child care expenses – in cash	yes	yes	40
Child care expenses – non-cash	yes	no	40
Counselling services – in cash	yes	yes	40
Counselling services – non-cash	yes	no	40
Disability-related employment benefits – in cash	yes	yes	40
Disability-related employment benefits – non-cash	yes	no	40
Discounts on merchandise and commissions on sales – non-cash	yes	no	40
Educational allowances for children – in cash	yes	yes	40
Employment insurance premium rebate – in cash	yes	yes	40
Gifts and awards – in cash	yes	yes	40
Gifts and awards – non-cash and near-cash	yes	no	40
Group term life insurance policies – employer-paid premiums – non-cash	yes	no	40
Housing allowance, clergy – in cash	[7]	yes	30
Housing allowance – in cash	yes	yes	30
Housing benefit, clergy, rent-free or low-rent – non cash	[7]	[9]	30
Housing benefit, rent-free or low-rent – non cash	yes	[9]	30
Housing loss – in cash	yes	yes	40
Interest-free and low-interest loans	yes	no	36
Loans – Home purchase	yes	no	36
Loans – Home relocation	yes	no	36
Loans – Forgiven – in cash	yes	yes	40
Meals – Overtime allowances – in cash	yes	yes	40
Meals – Overtime – in cash	yes	yes	40
Meals – Overtime – non-cash	yes	no	40
Meals – subsidized – non-cash	yes	no	40
Medical expenses – in cash	yes	yes	40
Medical expenses – non-cash	yes	no	40

Taxable allowance or benefit (continued)	Deduct CPP	Deduct EI	Code for T4 slip
Moving expenses and relocation benefits – in cash	yes	yes	40
Moving expenses and relocation benefits – non-cash	yes	no	40
Moving expenses – non-accountable allowance over $650 – in cash	yes	yes	40
Municipal officer's expense allowance	yes	no	40
Parking – in cash	yes	yes	40
Parking – non-cash	yes	no	40
Pooled registered pension plan contributions (paid to a plan not registered with the Minister of National Revenue)	yes	yes	40
Power saws and tree trimmers; rental paid by employer for employee-owned tools – in cash	yes	yes	40
Premiums for income maintenance plans and other insurance plans – non cash	yes	no	40
Premiums under provincial hospitalization, medical care insurance, and certain federal government plans – in cash	yes	yes	40
Premiums under provincial hospitalization, medical care insurance, and certain federal government plans – non-cash	yes	no	40
Professional membership dues – in cash	yes	yes	40
Professional membership dues – non-cash	yes	no	40
Recreational facilities (in house) – non-cash	yes	no	40
Recreational facilities or club membership dues – in cash	yes	yes	40
Registered retirement savings plan (RRSP) contributions – in cash	yes	12	40
Registered retirement savings plan (RRSP) administration fees – non-cash	yes	no	40
Scholarships and bursaries – in cash	yes	yes	40
Security option (cash-outs)	Yes	Yes	13
Security options	yes	no	13
Social events – in cash	yes	yes	40
Social events – non-cash	yes	no	40
Spouse or common-law partner's travelling expenses – in cash	yes	yes	40
Spouse or common-law partner's travelling expenses – non-cash	yes	no	40
Tax-Free Savings Account – contributions – in cash	yes	12	40
Tax-Free Savings Account – administration fees – non-cash	yes	no	40
Tickets	yes	no	40
Tool allowance – in cash	yes	yes	40
Tool reimbursement – in cash	yes	yes	40
Transportation passes – in cash	yes	yes	40
Transportation passes – non-cash	yes	no	40
Transportation to and from the job – in cash	yes	yes	40
Transportation to and from the job – non-cash	yes	no	40
Travel assistance in a prescribed zone – in-cash	yes	yes	32
Travel assistance in a prescribed zone – non-cash	yes	no	32
Travelling allowances other employees, unreasonable	yes	yes	40
Tuition fees – in cash	yes	yes	40
Tuition fees – non-cash	yes	no	40

Uniforms and protective clothing – in cash	yes	yes	40	yes
Uniforms and protective clothing – non-cash	yes	no	40	yes
Utilities allowance, clergy – in cash	7	yes	40	no
Utilities allowance – in cash	yes	yes	40	no
Utilities benefit, clergy – non cash	7	no	40	8
Utilities benefit, rent-free or low-rent – non cash	yes	no	40	8

[1] Except for security options, if a non-cash taxable benefit is the only form of remuneration you provide to your employee, there is no remuneration from which to withhold deductions. For more information, see "Calculate payroll deductions," on page 7.

[2] If no cash earnings are paid in a pay period, do not deduct EI premiums.

[3] Meals and short term accommodations are generally subject to the GST/HST. If taxable, include the GST/HST in the value of the benefit.

[4] Child care expenses are generally exempt of GST/HST. If taxable, include the GST/HST in the value of the benefit.

[5] Certain counselling services are subject to the GST/HST. If the services you pay are subject to the GST/HST, include the GST/HST in the value of the benefit.

[6] Disability-related employment benefits are generally taxable for GST/HST. If taxable, include the GST/HST in the value of the benefit.

[7] If you reduce the income used to calculate income tax deductions by the amount of the clergy residence deduction (including utilities), you may also reduce the pensionable earnings used to calculate CPP contributions by the same amount.

[8] Long-term accommodations are generally exempt of GST/HST and utilities are generally subject to the GST/HST. If taxable, include the GST/HST in the value of the benefit.

[9] If it is a non cash benefit, it is insurable if it is received by the employee in addition to cash earnings in a pay period. If no cash earnings are paid in the pay period, it is not insurable.

[10] Some medical expenses are subject to the GST/HST. For more information, see page 27.

Taxable Benefits

Taxable benefits are another form of employment remuneration.

Items the employer either <u>provides to an employee</u> (ex. a company-leased automobile given to the employee for both business and personal use) or <u>pays for on an employee's behalf</u> (ex. group term life insurance premiums).

When an employer provides employees with items that are to the <u>employee's benefit</u>, the Canada Revenue Agency (CRA) and Revenue Québec (RQ) may determine that the benefit is taxable to the employee.

NON-CASH TAXABLE BENEFITS

Non-cash taxable benefits are subject to statutory deductions for Canada/Québec Pension Plan (C/QPP) contributions, income tax, and Northwest Territories (NT)/Nunavut (NU) payroll tax.

Non-cash taxable benefits are <u>not considered insurable earnings</u> and are therefore not subject to Employment Insurance (EI) or Québec Parental Insurance Plan (QPIP) premiums.

NON-CASH OR NEAR CASH BENEFITS

Non-cash (or "in kind") benefit is the actual good, service, or property that you give to your employee. This includes a payment you make to a third party for the good or service if you are responsible for the expense.

Near-cash benefit is one that functions as cash, such as a <u>gift certificate or gift card</u>, or something that can easily be converted to cash, such as a <u>security, stock, or gold nugget</u>.

CPP – When a non-cash or near-cash benefit is taxable, it is also pensionable. This means you must deduct CPP contributions from the employee's pay. It also means that you must pay your employer's share of CPP to CRA.

EI – A taxable non-cash or near-cash benefit is generally <u>not insurable</u>. Do not deduct EI premiums.

Group Term Life Insurance

- Employers offer group term life insurance as part of their employee benefit package.
- Coverage is normally calculated as a multiple of the employee's annual salary rounded up to the nearest $1,000.
- The benefit is included in the employee's income as it is earned or enjoyed.

CALCULATING TAXABLE BENEFIT

The following formula calculates the employee's monthly taxable benefit:

Coverage amount = Annual salary x Coverage multiplier
(Round coverage amount up to nearest $1,000)

Ontario assesses Retail Sales Tax (RST) of 8% on all group insurance premiums, Manitoba assesses RST of 8% and Québec assesses a 9% tax.

Gifts

A gift or award that you give an employee is a <u>taxable</u> benefit from employment, whether it is cash, near-cash, or non-cash. However, some non-cash gifts and awards may be exempt.

Cash and near-cash gifts or awards are <u>always taxable and pensionable benefit</u> to the employee.

A near-cash item is not insurable earnings if it:

- Functions as cash, such as gift certificate or gift card
- An item that can be easily converted to cash, such as gold nuggets, securities, or stocks

For more information, see **rules for gifts and awards** and Policy for non-cash gifts and awards.

Examples of non-cash gifts or awards

Vouchers and event tickets are generally considered noncash gifts and awards. You give your employee a voucher (which may be a ticket or a certificate) that entitles the employee to receive an item for set value at a store.

> For example, you may give your employees a voucher for a Turkey valued up to $30 as a Christmas gift, and for convenience, you arrange for your employees to go to a particular grocery store and exchange the voucher for a Turkey. The employees <u>can only use the voucher to receive a turkey</u> valued up to $30 no substitutes.

A gift card or gift certificate to a movie theatre is not considered an event ticket. It is considered a **near-cash** gift or award.

With a gift card or gift certificate to a movie theatre, your employee can choose which movie to see and when to see it, or they can use the card or certificate at an arcade or concession stand.

Rules for Gifts and Awards

A **gift** must be for a special occasion such as a religious holiday, a birthday, a wedding, or the birth of a child.

An **award** must be for an employment-related accomplishment such as outstanding service or employees' suggestions. It is recognition of an employee's overall contribution to the workplace, not recognition of job performance. Generally, a valid, non-taxable award has clearly defined criteria, a nomination and evaluation process, and a limited number of recipients.

An award given to your employees for performance-related reasons (such as performing well in the job they were hired to do, exceeding production standards, completing a project ahead of schedule or under budget, putting in extra time to finish a project, covering a sick manager/colleague) is considered a **reward** and is a taxable benefit for the employee.

If you give your employee a non-cash gift or award for any other reason, this policy does not apply, and you must include the fair market value of the gift or award in the employee's income.

The gifts and awards policy does not apply to cash and near-cash items or to gifts or awards given to non-arm's length employees, such as your relatives, shareholders, or people related to them.

Policy for non-cash gifts and awards

- An unlimited number of non-cash gifts and awards with a combined total value of $500 or less annually.
- If the fair market value of the gifts and awards you give your employee is greater than $500, the amount over $500 must be included in the employee's income (ex. if you give gifts and awards with a total value of $650, there is a taxable benefit of $150 ($650 - $500).
- Items of small or trivial value do not have to be included when calculating the total value of gifts and awards given in the year for the purpose of the exemption. Examples of items of small or trivial value include:
  - Coffee or tea
  - T-shirts with employer's logos
  - Mugs
  - Plaques or trophies

Professional Membership Dues

If the business pays professional membership dues for the employee and the business is the primary beneficiary of the payment, there is no benefit for the employee.

If the business pays or reimburses professional membership dues because membership in the organization or association is a condition of employment, the business is the primary beneficiary, and there is no taxable benefit for the employee.

When membership is not a condition of employment, the employer is responsible for determining the primary beneficiary.

In all situations where the business pays or reimburses an employee's professional membership dues and the primary beneficiary is the employee, there is a taxable benefit for the employee.

REGISTERED RETIREMENT SAVINGS PLAN (RRSPs)

Employer contributions made to employee's RRSP and RRSP administration fees are a taxable benefit for the employee. If the GST/HST applies to the administration fees, include it in the value of the benefit.

Contributions the employer makes to the employee's RRSPs are generally paid in cash and are pensionable and insurable. Deduct CPP contributions and EI premiums.

However, employer contributions are considered non-cash benefits and are not insurable if your employees cannot withdraw the amounts from a group RRSP (except for withdrawals under the Home Buyer's Plan or Lifelong Learning Plan) before the employees retire or cease to be employed.

6. STATUTORY DEDUCTION

An employer may only deduct money from an employee's wages if they are legally required to do so or the employee approves the deduction in writing.

Legally required deductions include:

- Federal income tax
- Federal Employment Insurance premiums (EI)
- Canada Pension Plan contributions (CPP)
- A court order to garnish wages
-

If an employee agrees in writing, deductions can also include:
- Medical premiums
- Repayment of payroll advances
- Purchases made from an employer
- Accidental overpayments

*Reference:
https://www2.gov.bc.ca/gov/content/employment-business/employment-standards-advice/employment-standards/wages/deductions

Considerations:

When you calculate source deductions and contributions, you have to consider **all** of the following:

- The employee's situation
- Your situation as an employer or a payer
- The type of employment held by the employee
- The type of payment made
- The province of employment

*Reference:
https://www.canada.ca/en/revenue-agency/services/tax/businesses/topics/payroll/calculating-deductions/making-deductions.html

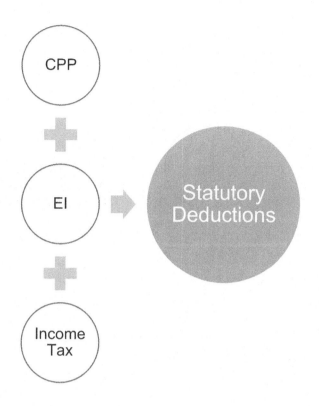

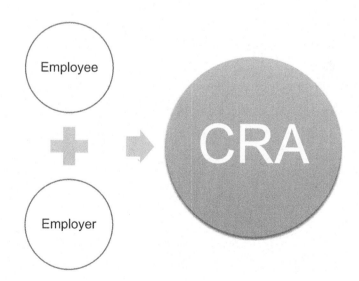

$$\text{Gross Pay} - \text{CPP} - \text{EI} - \text{Tax} = \text{Net Pay}$$

Employers are required to withhold and remit payroll deductions.

Statutory deductions order of Priority

- Canada/Quebec Pension Plan contributions
- Employment Insurance premiums
- Quebec Parental Insurance Plan Premiums
- Federal income tax
- Provincial income tax
- Northwest Territories and Nunavut income tax

7. CANADA PENSION PLAN

Canada Pension Plan (CPP)

CPP is a type of insurance plan which provides pension income for most Canadian employees or dependents benefits when they retire, disabled, or die.

Based on how much you have contributed and how long you have been making contributions from the time you become eligible

Pensionable earnings

Pensionable earnings are the employee's remuneration from pensionable office or employment with certain exceptions.

Generally, you must deduct CPP contributions from:

- Salary, wages or other remuneration
- Commissions
- Bonuses
- Most taxable benefits
- Honorariums
- Certain tips and gratuities

Pensionable Earnings

Special payments that are subject to Canada Pension Plan (CPP) deductions

Yes = included
No = excluded

Earnings	Pensionable
Bonuses and Incentive Pay	Yes
Commissions	Yes
Death Benefits	No
Directors' Fees - Fee Only	Yes
Directors' Fees - Fee in addition to salary	Yes/No[1]
Gratuities - controlled by employer	Yes
Gratuities - not controlled by employer	No
Honoraria by Virtue of employment or office	Yes
Gifts/Awards/Incentives (Taxable)	Yes
Overtime	Yes
Pension Payments or lump sum from pension	No
Profit-sharing Plan (EPSP)	No
Regular Pay/Salary	Yes
Retroactive pay and adjustment	Yes
Pay In Lieu	Yes
Retiring Allowance (Severance Pay)	No
Retirement Compensation Arrangement (RCA)	No
Sabbatical or Furlough Pay	Yes
Salary paid before/after WCB claim decided	Yes
Severance Pay	No
Shift Pay	Yes
Sick Pay (Accumulated sick leave credits paid after termination is not pensionable)	Yes
Statutory Holiday Pay	Yes
Supplementary Unemployment Benefits (HRSDC-approved SUB plans)	Yes
Taxable allowances	Yes
Tuition (in cash / non-cash)	Yes
Vacation pay	Yes
Wage-loss replacement benefits	Yes
WCB advances/WCB award	No
WCB top-up payments	Yes

Benefits (received with cash remuneration)	Pensionable
Automobile standby charge	Yes
Board and Lodging (if cash earnings also paid)	Yes
Employer contributions to RRSP	Yes
Group term life insurance	Yes
Interest-free and low interest loans	Yes
Provincial health insurance plans	Yes
Stock option benefits	Yes
Subsidized meals	No[2]
Gifts/Awards/Incentives	Yes

NOTES:
1. Whether or not to deduct CPP depends on the status of resident director's employment.
2. Dependent on how much of the meal cost is paid by the employee.

Are all employers required to contribute to pension plans?
Employer pension contributions are typically mandatory for government pension programs like CPP or QPP. Offering a private pension plan is at the employer's discretion, as are the terms of the plan within the employment contract.

payworks.ca

When to deduct CPP Contributions

- Age over 18 to age 69; after age 65 an employee may file with the employer a form to permit the discontinuance of contribution.
- If an employee is already receiving CPP disability benefits, do not deduct current earnings.

- <u>Determine if a benefit is taxable</u>
- <u>Determine the tax treatment of payments other than regular employment income</u>

When to stop deducting CPP contributions

Stop deducting CPP when the employee reaches the maximum contribution for the year in their employment with you.

- Maximum pensionable earnings CPP $68,500
- Maximum pensionable earnings CPP2 $73,200
- Basic exemption amount remains at $3,500.
- Annual maximum contributory earnings $65,000
- Annual maximum contributory earnings CPP2 $4,700
- CPP rate   5.95%
- Annual maximum contribution CPP $3,867.50
- Annual maximum contribution CPP2 $188.00

Reference:
https://www.canada.ca/en/revenue-agency/services/tax/businesses/topics/payroll/payroll-deductions-contributions/canada-pension-plan-cpp.html

Employer CPP contributions

You **must also contribute an amount equal** to the CPP contributions that you deduct from your employees' remuneration and remit the total of both amounts.

Employer matching

CPP Contribution

1:1

CPP FORMULA

Gross Earnings *(i.e. Salary, Overtime, Shift Premium)*

Plus +

Taxable benefits *((i.e., Life Insurance, Group RRSP, Gifts, stock options)*

Less -

non-taxable allowances*(i.e., safety shoe allowance – employer benefit)*

=

Pensionable Income

Less -

basic exemption

=

Net Pensionable Income

x

Multiply by the rate (**5.95%**)

=

CPP Deduction

CPP Rates

Year	Maximum annual pensionable earnings definition⑦	Basic exemption amount definition⑦	Maximum contributory earnings definition⑦	Employee and employer contribution rate (%) definition⑦	Maximum annual employee and employer contribution definition⑦
2024	$68,500	$3,500	$65,000	5.95	$3,867.50
2023	$66,600	$3,500	$63,100	5.95	$3,754.45
2022	$64,900	$3,500	$61,400	5.70	$3,499.80
2021	$61,600	$3,500	$58,100	5.45	$3,166.45
2020	$58,700	$3,500	$55,200	5.25	$2,898.00
2019	$57,400	$3,500	$53,900	5.10	$2,748.90

CPP Reference Chart

Pay Period Type	Basic Exemption	# Of Pays Per Year	Pay Period Exemption
Weekly	$3,500	52	$67.30
Biweekly	$3,500	26	$131.61
Semi-monthly	$3,500	24	$145.83
Monthly	$3,500	12	$291.66

Reference:

Employers' Guide – Payroll Deductions and Remittances - Canada.ca Publication T4001

https://www.canada.ca/en/revenue-agency/services/forms-publications/publications/t4001/employers-guide-payroll-deductions-remittances.html

How to calculate CPP – Manual calculation for CPP –

Reference:
https://www.canada.ca/en/revenue-agency/services/tax/businesses/topics/payroll/payroll-deductions-contributions/canada-pension-plan-cpp/manual-calculation-cpp.html

Sample Calculation:

Mary receives a semi-monthly pay of $1,575.00 from ABC Co. in BC, Calculate her CPP premium deduction.

= ($1,575 - $145.83) x 5.95%

= $1,429.17 x 5.95%

= $85.04

Anita is paid $1,850.00 biweekly from XZY Co. located in BC; XYZ company pays for $20/month premium for her group life. Calculate her CPP premium contribution

$20/month x 12 = $240/year ÷ 26 = $9.23 biweekly

$1,850.00 + 9.23 = $1,859.23 = Pensionable Earnings

1,859.23 -134.62 = 1,724.61 x 5.95% = 102.61 = CPP Contribution

Example

Joseph receives a weekly salary of $500 and $50 in taxable benefits. Calculate the amount of CPP contributions that you have to pay.

Step 1: Calculate the basic pay-period exemption
$3,500 ÷ 52 = $67.30 (do not round off)

Step 2: Calculate the total pensionable income
$500 + $50 = $550

Step 3: Deduct the basic pay-period exemption from the total pensionable income
$550 − $67.30 = $482.70

Step 4: Calculate the amount of CPP contributions
$482.70 × 5.70% = $27.51

Step 5: Calculate the amount of CPP contributions you have to pay
$27.51 × 2 = $55.02

Reference:
https://www.canada.ca/en/revenue-agency/services/tax/businesses/topics/payroll/payroll-deductions-contributions/canada-pension-plan-cpp/manual-calculation-cpp.html

What is the CPP enhancement

Before January 1, 2019, employees were making a contribution of 4.95% on their pensionable earnings up to their annual maximum pensionable earnings (first ceiling), with employers making an equal contribution. These are the **base contributions** to the CPP.

From 2019 to 2023, the contribution rate for employees increased gradually from 4.95% to 5.95%. These are the base contributions (4.95%) and the **first additional contribution** to the CPP (1%).

Beginning in 2024, a year's additional maximum pensionable earnings (second higher ceiling) is introduced. A **second additional CPP contribution (CPP2)** is made on these earnings, beginning at the first earnings ceiling and going up to the second earnings ceiling.

CPP2 contribution rates and maximums

Year	Additional maximum annual pensionable earnings definition⑦	Employee and employer contribution rate (%) definition⑦	Maximum annual employee and employer contribution definition⑦	Maximum annual self-employed contribution definition⑦
2025	$79,400 estimated figure	4%	$388 estimated figure	$776 estimated figure
2024	$73,200	4%	$188	$376

Pensionable and Insurable Earnings Review (PIER)

Each year CRA checks the calculations you made on the T4 slips that you filed with your T4 Summary.

CRA ensures that the pensionable and insurable earnings you reported correspond to the deductions you withheld and remitted.

If there is a deficiency between the CPP contributions or EI premiums required and those you reported, the amounts are listed on the PIER listing.

CRA will show the names of the affected employees, the figures we used in the calculations and the balance due.

You are responsible for remitting the balance due, including your employee's share.

For more information go to Guide T4001 Employers Guide – Chapter 4
https://www.canada.ca/en/revenue-agency/services/forms-publications/publications/t4001/employers-guide-payroll-deductions-remittances.html - P730_74100

8. EMPLOYMENT INSURANCE

Employment Insurance (EI)

Employment Insurance provides basic wage loss coverage for persons who have paid into the program.

- Administered by Service Canada
- Provides basic wage loss insurance for employees who are not receiving wages due to temporary layoff or loss of a job.
- Special benefits for workers who experience an interruption of earnings due to various life events such as illness, maternity, parental, compassionate care leaves.
- Maximum Benefit is 55% of your average weekly earnings up to $668 per week (from $650 in 2023)
- Maximum insurable earnings in 2024 are $63,200
- Employer contribution is 1.4 times the employee contribution

Reference:
https://www.canada.ca/en/services/benefits/ei/ei-regular-benefit/benefit-amount.html
https://www.canada.ca/en/employment-social-development/programs/ei.html
https://www.canada.ca/en/services/benefits/ei/ei-regular-benefit/eligibility.html

EI insurable earnings

Insurable earnings are the employee's earnings from insurable employment. **Insurable employment** includes most employment in Canada under a **contract of service**.

To be considered as insurable earnings, the amount has to be paid in cash by the person's employer and received and enjoyed by the person in respect of that employment.

Generally, you have to deduct EI premiums from:

- Salary, wages or other remuneration
- Commissions
- Bonuses
- Most taxable benefits received in cash
- Honorariums
- Certain tips and gratuities

Reference:
https://www.canada.ca/en/revenue-agency/services/tax/businesses/topics/payroll/payroll-deductions-contributions/employment-insurance-ei.html

EI Rates and Maximums

Federal EI premium rates and maximums

Year	Maximum annual insurable earnings definition⑦	Rate (%) definition⑦	Maximum annual employee premium definition⑦	Maximum annual employer premium definition⑦
2024	$63,200	1.66	$1,049.12	$1,468.77
2023	$61,500	1.63	$1,002.45	$1,403.43
2022	$60,300	1.58	$952.74	$1,333.84
2021	$56,300	1.58	$889.54	$1,245.36
2020	$54,200	1.58	$856.36	$1,198.90
2019	$53,100	1.62	$860.22	$1,204.31

Reference:
EI premium rates and maximums - Canada.ca
https://www.canada.ca/en/revenue-agency/services/tax/businesses/topics/payroll/payroll-deductions-contributions/employment-insurance-ei/ei-premium-rates-maximums.html

When to deduct EI Premiums

EI premiums:

| start to be deducted from the first dollar earned up to the yearly maximum | and | have **no age limit** for deducting them |

EI FORMULA

Gross Earnings - less non-taxable allowance (i.e., safety shoe allowance)

Calculating EI Premiums

https://www.canada.ca/en/revenue-agency/services/tax/businesses/topics/payroll/payroll-deductions-contributions/employment-insurance-ei/ei-premium-rate-maximum.html

Employer EI contributions

You **must also contribute 1.4 times the amount of** the EI premiums that you deduct from your employees' remuneration and remit the total of both amounts. Even if the required deductions were not made, you are **deemed** to have made them and the deductions not being made may result in a PIER.

Reduce EI Premiums

https://www.canada.ca/en/employment-social-development/programs/ei/ei-list/ei-employers/premium-reduction-program.html

Exercises:

Mary receives a semi-monthly pay of $1,575.00 from ABC Co. in BC, Calculate her EI premium Deduction and Employer EI Contribution

EI Employee Deductions:

$1,575 x 1.63% = $25.67

EI Employer Contribution:

$25.67 x 1.4 = $35.94

9. INCOME TAX

Federal income tax and provincial/territorial income taxes are calculated separately in Canada. Both are calculated on the same tax return, except for Quebec.

The income taxes are calculated based on taxable income. The tax rate increases as taxable income increases in each tax bracket.

After income taxes are calculated, non-refundable tax credits are deducted from the tax payable.

Tax Calculations

Payroll Deductions Online Calculator – PDOC

https://www.canada.ca/en/revenue-agency/services/e-services/e-services-businesses/payroll-deductions-online-calculator.html

Tax Deduction Tables

https://www.canada.ca/en/revenue-agency/services/forms-publications/payroll/t4032-payroll-deductions-tables.html

Section B - Canada Pension Plan contributions tables

- 52 pay periods a year (Weekly) [PDF]
- 26 pay periods a year (Biweekly) [PDF]
- 24 pay periods a year (Semi-monthly) [PDF]
- 12 pay periods a year (Monthly) [PDF]

Section C - Employment Insurance premiums tables

- When the <u>province or territory of employment is other than the province of Quebec [PDF]</u>

CALCULATING INCOME TAX

Gross Taxable Earnings = Gross Pay - Non-Taxable Allowance + Taxable Benefit

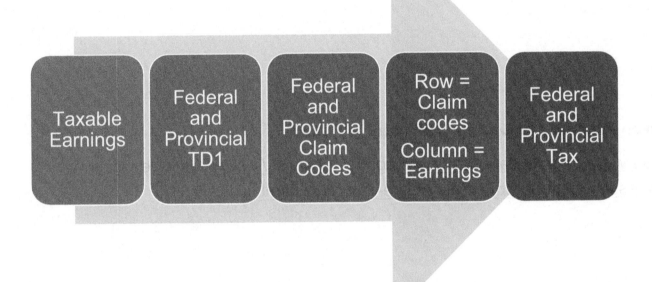

Other factors for determining taxable income on which you must deduct income tax.

- Deduction for a living in a prescribed zone
- Amount that a tax services office has authorized – Letter of Authority from CRA
- Employee's contributions to a Registered Pension Plan (RPP)
- Union dues (Québec has different rules)
- Employee's contributions to a Retirement Compensation Arrangement (RCA)
- Employee's and employer's contributions to a Registered Retirement Savings Plan (RRSP), provided you have reasonable grounds to believe the employee can deduct the contribution for the year.

Fundamental Canadian Payroll Administration

- Employee's contributions to a Pooled Registered Pension Plan (PRPP), or a similar Provincial Pension Plan, if the plan is registered with the Minister of National Revenue, and you have reasonable grounds to believe the employee can deduct the contributions for the year.

TD1 PERSONAL TAX CREDITS RETURN

- The TD1 Personal Tax Credit Returns are used to determine the amount of tax to be deducted from an individual's employment income or other income.

- Completed TD1 Personal Tax Credits Returns provide the appropriate tax code for which the applicable tax credit calculation can be determined. The basic personal exemption amount is the earnings not subject to taxation.

Canada Revenue Agency / Agence du revenu du Canada — **2023 Personal Tax Credits Return** — Protected B when completed — TD1

Read page 2 before filling out this form. Your employer or payer will use this form to determine the amount of your tax deductions.

Fill out this form based on the best estimate of your circumstances.

If you do not fill out this form, your tax deductions will only include the basic personal amount, estimated by your employer or payer based on the income they pay you.

Last name	First name and initial(s)	Date of birth (YYYY/MM/DD)	Employee number

Address	Postal code	For non-residents only Country of permanent residence	Social insurance number

1. Basic personal amount – Every resident of Canada can enter a basic personal amount of $15,000. However, if your net income from all sources will be greater than $165,430 and you enter $15,000, you may have an amount owing on your income tax and benefit return at the end of the tax year. If your income from all sources will be greater than $165,430, you have the option to calculate a partial claim. To do so, fill in the appropriate section of Form TD1-WS, Worksheet for the 2023 Personal Tax Credits Return, and enter the calculated amount here.

2. Canada caregiver amount for infirm children under age 18 – Only one parent may claim $2,499 for each infirm child born in 2006 or later who lives with both parents throughout the year. If the child does not live with both parents throughout the year, the parent who has the right to claim the "Amount for an eligible dependant" on line 8 may also claim the Canada caregiver amount for the child.

3. Age amount – If you will be 65 or older on December 31, 2023, and your net income for the year from all sources will be $42,335 or less, enter $8,396. You may enter a partial amount if your net income for the year will be between $42,335 and $98,309. To calculate a partial amount, fill out the line 3 section of Form TD1-WS.

TD1 Forms

https://www.canada.ca/en/revenue-agency/services/forms-publications/td1-personal-tax-credits-returns/td1-forms-pay-received-on-january-1-later.html

---

Fundamental Canadian Payroll Administration

Claim Codes – T4127

Chart 1 – 2023 Federal claim codes

Total claim amount ($) from	Total claim amount ($) to	Claim code
No claim amount	No claim amount	0
0.00	15,000.00	1
15,000.01	17,583.00	2
17,583.01	20,166.00	3
20,166.01	22,749.00	4
22,749.01	25,332.00	5
25,332.01	27,915.00	6
27,915.01	30,498.00	7
30,498.01	33,081.00	8
33,081.01	35,664.00	9
35,664.01	38,247.00	10

Provincial Claim Codes

Chart 2 – 2023 British Columbia claim codes

Total claim amount ($) from	Total claim amount ($) to	Claim code
No claim amount	No claim amount	0
0.00	11,981.00	1
11,981.01	14,677.00	2
14,677.01	17,373.00	3
17,373.01	20,069.00	4
20,069.01	22,765.00	5
22,765.01	25,461.00	6
25,461.01	28,157.00	7
28,157.01	30,853.00	8
30,853.01	33,549.00	9
33,549.01	36,245.00	10

Fundamental Canadian Payroll Administration

Tax Tables

https://www.canada.ca/en/revenue-agency/services/forms-publications/payroll/t4032-payroll-deductions-tables/t4032bc-jan.html

Federal tax deductions
Effective January 1, 2023
Biweekly (26 pay periods a year)
Also look up the tax deductions in the provincial table

Pay From	Less than	CC 0	CC 1	CC 2	CC 3	CC 4	CC 5	CC 6	CC 7	CC 8	CC 9	CC 10
1329	1345	178.70	92.15	84.70	69.80	54.90	40.00	25.10	10.20			
1345	1361	180.90	94.35	86.90	72.00	57.10	42.20	27.30	12.40			
1361	1377	183.10	96.60	89.15	74.25	59.35	44.45	29.55	14.65			
1377	1393	185.35	98.80	91.35	76.45	61.55	46.65	31.75	16.85	1.95		
1393	1409	187.55	101.00	93.55	78.65	63.75	48.85	33.95	19.05	4.15		
1409	1425	189.80	103.25	95.80	80.90	66.00	51.10	36.20	21.30	6.40		
1425	1441	192.00	105.45	98.00	83.10	68.20	53.30	38.40	23.50	8.60		
1441	1457	194.20	107.70	100.25	85.35	70.40	55.50	40.60	25.70	10.80		
1457	1473	196.45	109.90	102.45	87.55	72.65	57.75	42.85	27.95	13.05		
1473	1489	198.65	112.10	104.65	89.75	74.85	59.95	45.05	30.15	15.25	.35	
1489	1505	200.85	114.35	106.90	92.00	77.10	62.20	47.25	32.35	17.45	2.55	
1505	1521	203.10	116.55	109.10	94.20	79.30	64.40	49.50	34.60	19.70	4.80	
1521	1537	205.30	118.75	111.30	96.40	81.50	66.60	51.70	36.80	21.90	7.00	
1537	1553	207.55	121.00	113.55	98.65	83.75	68.85	53.95	39.05	24.15	9.20	
1553	1569	209.75	123.20	115.75	100.85	85.95	71.05	56.15	41.25	26.35	11.45	

Tax Bracket

TaxTips.ca - Canadian Tax Rates - Federal										
	Canada 2023 Marginal Tax Rates					Canada 2022 Marginal Tax Rates				
2023 Taxable Income	Other Income	Capital Gains	Canadian Dividends		2022 Taxable Income	Other Income	Capital Gains	Canadian Dividends		
			Eligible	Non-Eligible				Eligible	Non-Eligible	
first $53,359	15.00%	7.50%	-0.03%	6.87%	first $50,197	15.00%	7.50%	-0.03%	6.87%	
over $53,359 up to $106,717	20.50%	10.25%	7.56%	13.19%	over $50,197 up to $100,392	20.50%	10.25%	7.56%	13.19%	
over $106,717 up to $165,430	26.00%	13.00%	15.15%	19.52%	over $100,392 up to $155,625	26.00%	13.00%	15.15%	19.52%	
over $165,430 up to $235,675	29.32%	14.66%	19.73%	23.34%	over $155,625 up to $221,708	29.38%	14.69%	19.81%	23.41%	
over $235,675	33.00%	16.50%	24.81%	27.57%	over $221,708	33.00%	16.50%	24.81%	27.57%	

Marginal tax rate for dividends is a % of actual dividends received (not grossed-up taxable amount).
Marginal tax rate for capital gains is a % of total capital gains (not taxable capital gains).
Gross-up rate for eligible dividends is 38%, and for non-eligible dividends is 15%.
For more information see dividend tax credits.
Copyright © 2002-2023 Boat Harbour Investments Ltd.

TaxTips.ca Federal Basic Personal Amount			
2023 Personal Amount	2023 Tax Rate	2022 Personal Amount	2022 Tax Rate
$15,000	15%	$14,398	15%

Reference: https://www.taxtips.ca/taxrates/canada.htm

Gross to Net Steps

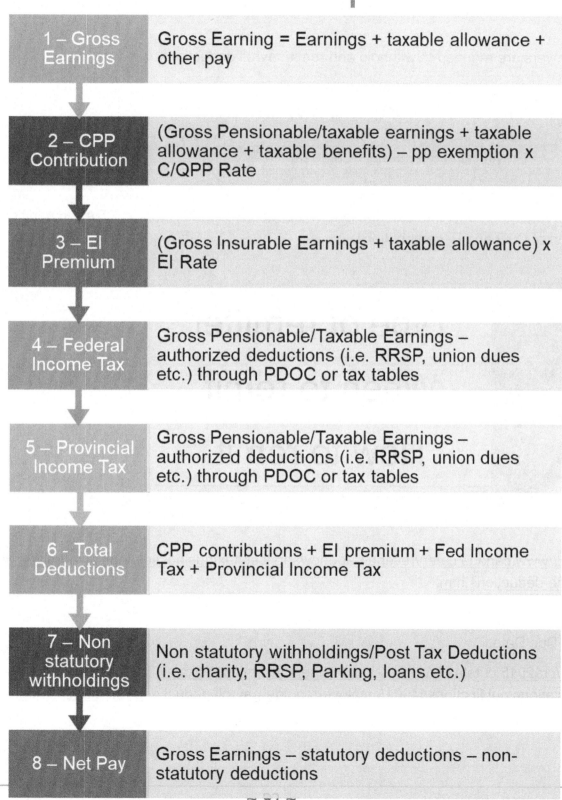

1 – Gross Earnings	Gross Earning = Earnings + taxable allowance + other pay
2 – CPP Contribution	(Gross Pensionable/taxable earnings + taxable allowance + taxable benefits) – pp exemption x C/QPP Rate
3 – EI Premium	(Gross Insurable Earnings + taxable allowance) x EI Rate
4 – Federal Income Tax	Gross Pensionable/Taxable Earnings – authorized deductions (i.e. RRSP, union dues etc.) through PDOC or tax tables
5 – Provincial Income Tax	Gross Pensionable/Taxable Earnings – authorized deductions (i.e. RRSP, union dues etc.) through PDOC or tax tables
6 - Total Deductions	CPP contributions + EI premium + Fed Income Tax + Provincial Income Tax
7 – Non statutory withholdings	Non statutory withholdings/Post Tax Deductions (i.e. charity, RRSP, Parking, loans etc.)
8 – Net Pay	Gross Earnings – statutory deductions – non-statutory deductions

10. REMITTANCE

Employers are required to withhold and remit payroll deductions.

- Canada Pension Plan contributions
- Employment Insurance premiums
- Federal income tax
- Provincial and territorial income tax

Employers must remit these deductions to Canada Revenue Agency (CRA), in addition to their portion of CPP and EI contributions.

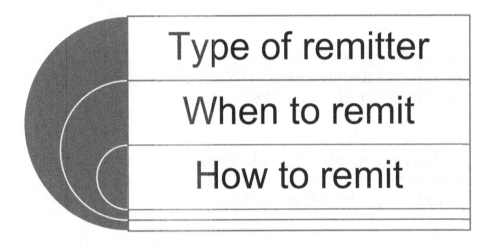

https://www.canada.ca/en/revenue-agency/services/tax/businesses/topics/payroll/remitting-source-deductions.html

CRA Due Dates

http://cra2018.cutetax.com/en/revenue-agency/services/forms-publications/publications/t4001/employers-guide-payroll-deductions-remittances.html

Remittance thresholds for employer source deductions

Remitter types	AMWA[1]	Due dates
Regular remitter	Less than $25,000	We have to **receive** your deductions on or before the 15th day of the month after the month you paid your employees.
Quarterly remitter	Less than $1,000[2] and less than $3,000	If you are eligible for quarterly remitting, we have to **receive** your deductions on or before the 15th day of the month immediately following the end of each quarter. The quarters are: ■ January to March ■ April to June ■ July to September ■ October to December The due dates are April 15, July 15, October 15, and January 15.
Accelerated remitter threshold 1	$25,000 to $99,999.99	We have to **receive** your deductions by the following dates: ■ For remuneration paid in the first 15 days of the month, remittances are due by the 25th day of the same month. ■ For remuneration paid from the 16th to the end of the month, remittances are due by the 10th day of the following month.
Accelerated remitter threshold 2	$100,000 or more	You have to remit your deductions through a Canadian financial institution so that we **receive** them within three working days following the last day of the following pay periods: ■ the 1st through the 7th day of the month ■ the 8th through the 14th day of the month ■ the 15th through the 21st day of the month ■ the 22nd through the last day of the month

1. Average monthly withholding amount
2. This is a monthly withholding amount (MWA), not an AMWA. For more information, go to Chapter 8 starting on page 49.

Average monthly withholding amount (AMWA)

When the due date falls on a Saturday, a Sunday, or a public holiday recognized by the CRA, we consider your payment to be on time if we receive it on the next business day. For a list of public holidays, go to Public holidays.

Remittance forms:

- Form PD7A, Statement of Account for Current Source Deductions,
  for regular and quarterly remitters for accelerated remitters
- Form PD7A(TM), Statement of Account for Current Source Deductions,
  or Form PD7A-RB, Remittance voucher for current source deductions,

Failure to Comply

A. Failure to Deduct

If you fail to deduct the required CPP contributions or EI premiums or Income Tax, you are responsible for these amounts even if you cannot recover the amounts from the employee.

CRA will assess you for both the employer's share and the employee's share of any contributions and premiums owing plus penalties. The CRA will apply a penalty <u>and</u> charge interest.

A penalty is assessed when the required CPP, EI, and income tax were not deducted. The penalty is:

10% of the amounts that were not deducted	or	20% of the amounts that were not deducted for a second or additional failures in a calendar year, if they were made knowingly or under circumstances of gross negligence

CRA can assess a penalty of 10% of the amount of CPP, EI, and Income Tax not deducted. If you are assessed this penalty more than once in a calendar year, a 20% penalty will apply to the second or later failures if they were made knowingly or under circumstances of gross negligence.

The interest rates are announced in the month preceding each calendar quarter.

*Reference:
https://www.canada.ca/en/revenue-agency/services/tax/businesses/topics/payroll/calculating-deductions/making-deductions.html

Interest

If you do not pay an amount that is due, the CRA may apply interest from the day the payment was due.

The CRA sets the interest rate for every calendar quarter, based on prescribed interest rates	and	The interest is compounded daily	and	The CRA applies interest to late payment of assessed penalties

The interest rates are announced in the month preceding each calendar quarter.

Reference:

https://www.canada.ca/en/revenue-agency/services/tax/businesses/topics/payroll/calculating-deductions/making-deductions.html

B. Failure to Remit

Payments made on the due date but not at a financial institution can be charged a penalty of 3% of the amount due.

Penalty applies on either of the following:

- You deduct the amounts, but do not send them to CRA
- You deduct the amounts, but send them to CRA late

The penalties are as follows:

3% if the amount is one to three days late

5% if it is four or five days late

7% if it is six or seven days late

10% if it is more than seven days late, or if no amount is remitted

Interest Charges:

- If you do not pay an amount that is due, CRA may apply interest from the day your payment was due
- Interest is compounded daily

Convictions:

- If the employer does not comply with the deducting, remitting, and reporting requirements, the employer may be prosecuted.
- Fines can range from $1,000 to $25,000, or fines may be imposed, and imprisonment recommended for a term of up to 12 months.

Director's Liability:

If a corporation does not deduct, remit, or pay amounts (CPP, EI, and Income Tax), the director(s) of the corporation are liable along with the corporation, to pay the amount due.

Reference:

Consequences of non-compliance

https://www.canada.ca/en/revenue-agency/services/tax/businesses/topics/payroll/penalties-interest-other-consequences/consequences-non-compliance.html

CRA - Penalties

https://www.canada.ca/en/revenue-agency/services/tax/businesses/topics/payroll/penalties-interest-other-consequences/payroll-penalties-interest.html

PIER Assessment

Pensionable Insurance and Earnings Report

- Each year, the CRA checks the calculations you made on the T4 slips that you filed with your T4 summary.
- CRA ensures that the pensionable and insurable earnings you reported correspond to the deductions you withheld and remitted.
- If there is a deficiency between the CPP contributions or EI premiums required and those you reported, the amounts are listed on the PIER listing.
- CRA will show the names of the affected employees, the figures we used in the calculations, and the balance due.
- **Employers are responsible for remitting the balance due, including the employee's share.**

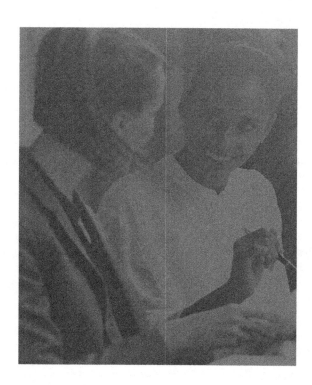

11. NON-STATUTORY WITHOLDINGS

Non-Statutory Withholdings

<u>Garnishment Order:</u>

When an individual in Canada fails to pay an obligation to another party then that party can file a claim with the courts.

If the court finds in favor with the claimant and the individual does not immediately make payment, then the court can issue a Garnishment Order.

How Wage Garnishment is used to collect your debts

Employer Compulsory Withholdings:

- Union Dues
- Premiums for group insurance
- Loan payments
- Social Fund for employees

Employer Optional Deductions:

- Parking fees
- Charities
- Employer sponsored plans
- Employer sponsored funds

Employer Paid Premiums

- Canada Pension Plan contributions
- Employment Insurance premiums
- Workers' Compensation, WorksafeBC
- Employer Health Tax, BC

Workers' Compensation

Each Province and territory administer WC insurance, including:

- Premium rates
- Assessable earnings
- Industry classification
- Schedules of required payment of premiums
- Registration processes for employers
- Benefit amounts for eligible employees
- Return to Work programs for injured workers
- Programs to encourage employers to develop safe work practices, education and training of employees.

Although there may be exceptions, generally the gross taxable and pensionable earnings reported on the T4 slip will be the assessable earnings for the calculation of premiums.

Provincial Max Assessable Earnings

BC Workers Compensation Maximum Assessable Earnings for year 2024 is $116,700.

Reference:
https://www.worksafebc.com/en/law-policy/claims-rehabilitation/compensation-related-maximum-wage-rates

Workers Compensation Assessable Earnings (continued on next page)

The portion of an employee's income that is used to calculate the premiums or contributions an employer must pay to the workers' compensation board

Yes = included
No = excluded

	BC	AB	SK	MB	ON	QC	NB	PE	NS	NL	YT	NT	NU
Allowances (taxable)	Yes[1]	Yes	Yes	Yes	Yes	Yes	No	Yes	Yes	Yes	Yes	Yes	Yes
Benefits (taxable)													
Board and lodging	Yes[13]	Yes	Yes	Yes	Yes	Yes	No	Yes	Yes	Yes	Yes	Yes	Yes
Interest free loans	No	Yes	Yes	Yes	Yes	Yes	No	No	Yes	Yes	Yes	Yes	Yes
Employer provided auto	Yes	Yes	Yes	Yes	Yes	Yes	No	Yes	Yes	Yes	Yes	Yes	Yes
Life insurance	Yes	Yes	Yes[4]	Yes	Yes	Yes	No	Yes	Yes	Yes	Yes	Yes	Yes
Private health care	No	No	Yes	No	No	Yes	No	No	No	No	No	No	No
Employer RRSP Contributions	Yes	Yes	Yes	Yes	Yes[2]	Yes	Yes	No	Yes	Yes	Yes	Yes	Yes
Stock options	Yes	Yes	Yes	Yes	Yes[2]	Yes	No	No	Yes	Yes	Yes	Yes	Yes
Earnings (taxable)													
Bonuses (paid in cash)	Yes	Yes	Yes	Yes	Yes	Yes	Yes	Yes	Yes	Yes	Yes	Yes	Yes
Call-in/back Pay	Yes	Yes	Yes	Yes	Yes[2]	Yes	Yes	Yes	Yes	Yes	Yes	Yes	Yes
Commissions	Yes	Yes	Yes	Yes	Yes	Yes	Yes	Yes	Yes	Yes	Yes	Yes	Yes
Director's fees	Yes	No	Yes	Yes	Yes	No	Yes	No	Yes	Yes	Yes	No	No
Gifts (cash/kind)	Yes[6]	Yes[2]	Yes	Yes	Yes[2]	Yes[2]	Yes	Yes[2]	Yes	Yes	Yes	Yes	Yes
Long-term disability (employer paid)	Yes	Yes	Yes[5]	Yes	Yes	Yes[12]	Yes	Yes[11]	No	Yes[2]	Yes	Yes	Yes
Maternity leave	Yes	Yes	Yes	Yes	Yes	Yes	Yes	Yes	No	Yes	Yes	Yes	Yes
Pre-retirement leave/earnings	Yes	No	Yes	No	No[7]	Yes	No	Yes	Yes	Yes	Yes	No	No
Salary/wages/overtime pay	Yes	Yes	Yes	Yes	Yes	Yes	Yes	Yes	Yes	Yes	Yes	Yes	Yes
Severance pay/retiring allowance	No	No	No	Yes	No	No	No	No	No	No	No	No	No
Shift premium	Yes	Yes	Yes	Yes	Yes	Yes	Yes	Yes	Yes	Yes	Yes	Yes	Yes
Short-term disability (employer paid)	Yes	Yes	Yes[5]	Yes	Yes	Yes[12]	Yes	Yes[11]	No	Yes[2]	Yes	Yes	Yes
Sick pay	Yes	Yes	Yes[8]	Yes	Yes	Yes[12]	Yes	Yes	Yes	Yes[9]	Yes	Yes	Yes

Workers Compensation Assessable Earnings (continued)

Yes = included
No = excluded

	BC	AB	SK	MB	ON	QC	NB	PE	NS	NL	YT	NT	NU
Sick pay (on termination)	No	No	No	No	Yes	No	No	No	No	Yes	No	Yes	Yes
Standby pay	Yes	Yes	Yes	Yes	Yes	Yes	Yes	Yes	Yes	Yes	Yes	Yes	Yes
Temporary lay-off	Yes	Yes	No	Yes	Yes	Yes	Yes	Yes	Yes	Yes	Yes	Yes	Yes
Tips/gratuities	Yes[3]	Yes	Yes	Yes[3]	Yes	Yes	Yes[2]	Yes[2]	Yes[2]	Yes[2]	Yes	Yes	Yes
Vacation pay/paid stat holidays	Yes	Yes	Yes	Yes	Yes	Yes	Yes	Yes	Yes	Yes	Yes	Yes	Yes
Wages in lieu of notice/Indemnity	No	Yes	Yes	Yes	Yes	Yes	Yes	Yes[2]	Yes	Yes	Yes	Yes	Yes
WCB award	Yes	No	No	No	No	No	No	No	No	No	No	No	No
WCB top-up	Yes	Yes	Yes	Yes	N/A	Yes	Yes	Yes	Yes	No[10]	Yes	Yes	Yes

NOTES
1. Not assessable if employer requests ruling.
2. When taxable.
3. When documentation exists in employee records.
4. If total premium paid by employer.
5. First 3 months included only.
6. Gifts in cash only.
7. When worker using sick pay credits remains on employer payroll until retirement (sick pay credit terminate).
8. Amounts paid not exceeding 3 months absence included. Amounts exceeding 3 months excluded entirely.
9. Up to 13 consecutive weeks.
10. Not permitted.
11. When reported as income.
12. First 105 sick days only.
13. Where the board and lodging are the principal form of remuneration they would be considered as assessable.

WCB Maximum Assessable Earnings

Province	Filing Deadline	WCB Maximum Assessable Earnings
BC	Last day of February (quarterly) March 1-15 (yearly)	$116,700
AB	February 28	$104,600
SK	February 28	$99,945
MB	February 28	$160,510
ON	Last day of March	$112,500
QC	Before March 15	$94,000
NB	February 28	$82,100
PE	February 28	$78,400
NS	February 28	$72,500
NL	February 28	$76,955
YT	Last day of February	$102,017
NT	February 28	$110,600
NU	February 28	$110,600

Employer Health Tax - BC

Employers with B.C. remuneration:

- Of $500,000 (exemption amount) or less don't pay employer health tax

- Between $500,000.01 and $1,500,000 (notch rate amount) pay the reduced tax amount as calculated:

    - 2.925% x (B.C. remuneration - $500,000)

- Greater than $1,500,000 pay the tax on their total B.C. remuneration as calculated:

    - 1.95% x total B.C. remuneration

Employer health tax B.C. remuneration - Province of British Columbia (gov.bc.ca) - LINK

12. TERMINATION OF EMPLOYMENT

Being terminated from employment means someone is no longer working for an employer. The decision to terminate may be made by the worker, or by the employer.

Voluntary Termination

An employee who chooses to end working for an employer voluntarily terminates their job. Reasons for choosing to leave their employer may include:

- Finding another job and/or relocating
- Returning to school
- Resignation
- Retirement

Involuntary Termination

Involuntary termination results from an employer terminating work for an employee. Situations when this may occur are:

- Shortage of work
- Company downsizing
- Events beyond the control of the employer

Involuntary terminations may also be a result of the conduct of an employee, resulting in **termination with cause.**

- Poor performance or incompetence
- Misconduct or unethical behavior

Typically, employers have established policies and opportunities for issues to be addressed, prior to termination.

Employee-Employer Relationship

Is deemed to exist where any one of the following four statements is true:

- The employee retains the right to be recalled for work
- There is an expectation of work to be performed by the employee
- The employee continues to accrue benefits in the organization's pension plan
- The employee continues to participate in all the benefit plans that were available while they were employed

Period of Notice

To end an employee's job, employers can give written working notice, or an equal amount of pay called compensation for length of service. They can also choose to give a combination of both notice and pay.

There are certain limited exceptions when an employer will not be required to pay compensation for length of service.

Employers can also fire an employee for just cause. If an employer has just cause, they don't have to give notice or pay.

Employers can write to an employee to let them know their job will end by a certain date. Employees must be able to work and earn income for the duration of the notice period. Notice cannot begin if an employee is:

- On vacation
- On leave
- On temporary layoff
- On strike or lockout
- Unavailable for work due to medical reasons

Pay In Lieu of Notice

Employers must wait for an employee to return to work before they can give notice. If an employer can't give notice (for example, the employee is on vacation, leave or temporary layoff) they can pay compensation instead.

If an employee continues to work after a notice period ends, the notice is cancelled. The employee is still employed, and the employer must give a notice again or pay compensation to end the job.

Once an employer gives written notice, they can't change the job without the employee's written agreement (for example, lowering hours or pay).

Compensation for Length of Service

Employers can pay employees money to compensate for the loss of their job. This means an employer can let an employee go immediately if they want if they pay the entire compensation required.

Calculating pay and/or notice required

The amount of written notice and/or pay is based on how long an employee has been employed.

Amount of written notice and/or pay required

Length of employment	Amount required
Three months or less	No notice and/or pay
More than three months	One week of notice and/or pay
More than one year	Two weeks of notice and/or pay
More than three years	Three weeks of notice and/or pay, plus one week of notice/pay after each additional year of employment (to a maximum of eight weeks)

Example: An employee has worked for a company for two years and their job is going to end. The employer can choose to do one of the following:
- Give the employee two weeks of written working notice.
- Pay the employee for two weeks and let them go immediately.
- Give the employee one week of working notice and one week of pay.

The sale, lease or transfer of a business does not interrupt an employee's length of employment unless the employee has been properly terminated by the seller's employer before the transfer of the business occurs.

Severance Pay

Severance pay is money your employer pays you when you lose your job through no fault of your own.

Your employer may call it a severance package, severance agreement or retiring allowance.

The federal, provincial, and territorial governments make regulations about severance pay. In some cases, you may not be eligible for severance pay. For example, you may not be eligible for severance pay if you've worked for your employer for only a short time.

To find out what severance pay to expect, review documents that outline your salary and terms of dismissal.

Severance pay is **not** considered employment income.

Calculating a week's pay

To calculate a week's pay, **divide** total wages earned by the employee over the last eight weeks by eight.

Include all wages – this includes salary, commission, statutory holiday pay and paid vacation. **Don't include overtime.**

If an employee is laid off, they're still considered to be employed. Include the time an employee was temporarily laid off when calculating their length of employment.

Ending employment while on temporary layoff

If an employee's job ends while they're temporarily laid off, include the layoff period when calculating their length of employment. **An employee on layoff is still considered to be employed.**

When calculating a week's pay, use the eight-week period immediately before the layoff began.

Vacation Pay on Termination

Vacation pay that is calculated as a percentage or fraction of their vacationable earnings during their period of employment, less any vacation pays already paid. Vacation payments made on termination of employment are considered income from employment.

This pay is considered income from employment and is subject to all statutory deductions. If the vacation pay is paid with the final pay period earnings, and regular deductions for C/QPP apply. If it is paid separately, no pay period exemption is applied.

Under the employment/labour standards, the following payments are required on termination of employment:

- Wages in lieu of notice
- Vacation pays
- Severance pays

Employee not entitled to Severance Pay

- Quits, retires, or is fired for just cause
- Has not been employed for three consecutive months
- Works on an on-call basis doing temporary assignments
- Cannot perform the work because of an unforeseeable event or circumstance
- Is employed at one or more construction sites for an employer whose main business is construction
- Refuses reasonable alternative work
- Is a teacher employed by a board of school trustees?
- Is hired for a definite term (with set start and end dates) or for specific work to be completed in 12 months or less

Payment Deadlines: Paying Final Wages

Final wages are everything the employer owes an employee. It may include regular wages, overtime, statutory holiday pay, compensation for length of service and vacation pay. Final payment must be made:

- Within **48 hours** after the last day an employee works when an **employer** ends employment
- Within **six days** after the employee's last day of work when an **employee** quits
-

If an employee cannot be located, the employer must pay the wages to the Director of Employment Standards within 60 days of the wages being payable. The Director holds the wages in trust for the employee.

Lump Sum Tax Rates

Retiring allowances are treated as lump-sum payments. Income tax is deducted, unless it is paid directly into a RRSP or RPP.

LUMP-SUM PAYMENT (NON-QUÉBEC)	COMBINED FEDERAL/PROVINCIAL TAX RATES
Up to $5,000.00	10%
$5,000.01 to $15,000.00	20%
$15,000.01 and over	30%

13. RECORD OF EMPLOYMENT (ROE)

A record of employment (ROE) provides information on employment history.

The ROE is the form—whether electronic or paper—those employers complete for employees receiving **insurable earnings** who stop working and experience an **interruption of earnings**. The ROE is the single most important document in the Employment Insurance (EI) program.

A ROE must be completed even if the employee does not intend to apply for EI benefits.

There are two ROE formats available: an ROE may be transmitted **electronically** or can be a completed **paper** ROE form.

Interruption of earnings

Occurs when

- An employee goes seven (7) consecutive calendar days without both work and insurable earnings from the employer, OR
- An employee's salary falls below 60% of regular weekly earnings because of illness, injury, quarantine, pregnancy, the need to care for a newborn or a child placed for the purposes of adoption, or the need to provide care or support of a family member who is gravely ill with a significant risk of death, OR
- When requested by Service Canada
- When the organization changes its pay period frequency
- When there is a change in ownership with no actual break in work

Part-Time, On-Call, or Casual Workers

A Record of Employment does **not** need to be issued each time; however, an ROE must be issued in any of the following situations:

- The ROE is requested by the employee and an interruption of earnings has occurred
- The employee is no longer on the employer's active employment list
- The ROE is requested by Service Canada
- The employee did not work or earn any insurable earnings for a period of 30 calendar days

Filing the ROE

The Record of Employment can be completed manually or electronically.

The employer must issue an ROE within **5 calendar days** after the end of the pay period in which an employee's interruption of earnings occurs or the date, they become aware of the interruption.

Employers must communicate with the Employer Contact Center to order ROE forms in paper. These 3-part forms are assigned to the Employer payroll account and are not transferable to another company.

Filing the ROE electronically can be done in a few different ways:

- Through ROE Web using a compatible payroll software to upload ROEs from the organization's payroll system.
- Through ROE Web by manually entering data online through Service Canada's website.
- Through Secure Automated Transfer (SAT), which may be performed by a payroll service provider on a client's behalf using bulk transfer technology.

When filing electronically, employers with a weekly, biweekly, or semi-monthly pay cycle have **5 calendar days** after the <u>end of the pay period</u> in which there was an interruption of earnings to issue the ROE.

If the pay cycle is monthly, or every four weeks, employers must issue electronic ROEs the earlier of:

- Up to five (5) calendar days after the end of the pay period when the interruption of earnings begins.
- Up to **15 calendar days** after the first day of the interruption of earnings.

BLOCK BY BLOCK INSTRUCTIONS FOR COMPLETING THE ROE

Block	Information	Details
1	Serial Number	• Pre-printed (manual) • Auto generated (electronically)
2	Serial Number of ROE amended or replaced	• Completed only if issuing an amended ROE
3	Employer's payroll reference number (optional)	• The number used to identify employees in your payroll records
4	Employer's name and address	• The same name and address that appear on the CRA remittance form used to report your payroll
5	CRA Business Number (Payroll Program Account Number)	• The Canada Revenue Agency Payroll Account Number used to report the employee's payroll deductions to CRA • Consists of 9 numbers followed, by 2 letters, followed by four numbers
6	Pay period type	• Weekly • Biweekly • Semi monthly • Monthly • 13 pay periods a year
7	Postal code	• Employer's postal code
8	Social Insurance Number	• Employee's Social Insurance Number
9	Employee's name and address	• Employee's name and number you have on file
10	First day worked	• Employee's first day of work • First day employee worked after the last interruption of earnings
11	Last day for which paid	• Last day for which employee received insurable earnings • If calculating based on Salary Continuance, enter the last day of this period, **not** the last day worked
12	Final pay period ending date	• The end date of the final pay period that includes the date entered in Block 11 • Can never be earlier than the date in Block 11
13	Occupation (Optional)	• An accurate description of the employee's main occupation
14	Expected date of recall	• If the employee is returning, enter the date if it is known, or check the "Unknown" box

Block	Information	Details
	(Optional)	• If the employee will not be returning, check the "Not returning" box

Block	Information	Details
15A	Total insurable hours	**Three Steps:** • Determine the number of consecutive pay periods to use • Determine which hours are insurable • Calculate the employee's total insurable hours **Pay Period Type:** • Weekly.......................... 53 • Biweekly........................ 27 • Semi-monthly................. 25 • Monthly......................... 13 • 13 pay periods a year....... 14
15B	Total insurable earnings	**Three Steps:** • Determine the number of consecutive pay periods to use • Determine which earnings are insurable • Calculate the employee's total insurable earnings **Pay Period Type:** • Weekly.......................... 27 • Biweekly........................ 14 • Semi-monthly................. 13 • Monthly......................... 7 • 13 pay periods a year........ 7
15C	Insurable earnings by pay period	**If completing by paper:** • Complete only if there was a break in employment **Pay Period Type:** • Weekly – last 27* pay periods • Biweekly – last 14* pay periods • Semi-monthly – last 13* pay periods • Monthly – last 7* pay periods • 13 pay periods a year – last 7* pay periods *Or less if period of employment is shorter **If completing electronically:** • Must be completed regardless of if there was a break in employment.

		• The most recent pay period is entered in under "P.P. 1"
		Pay Period Type:
		• Weekly – last 53* pay periods.
		• Biweekly – last 27* pay periods.
		• Semi-monthly – last 25* pay periods.
		• Monthly – last 13* pay periods.
		• 13 pay periods a year – last 14* pay periods.
		*Or less if period of employment is shorter

Block	Information	Details
16	Reason for issuing this ROE	• A – Shortage of work (end of contract/season, end of casual/part-time work, end of school year, shutdown of operations, organization restructuring) • B – Strike or lock-out • C – Return to school (this code is being phased out) • D – Illness or injury • E – Quit • F – Maternity • G – Retirement because of mandatory retirement • E – Voluntary retirement • H – Work sharing • J – Apprentice training • M – Dismissal • N – Leave of absence • P – Paternal • Z – Compassionate care • K – Other (used only in exceptional circumstances: change in payroll/ownership/organization name, change in pay period type, death of an employee, Service Canada requested ROE – must include an explanation in Block 18)
17	Separation payments	Payments or benefits (other than regular pay) paid in or in anticipation of the final pay period, or payable later • 17A – Vacation Pay • 17B – Statutory Holiday Pay • 17C – Other Monies (ex. severance)
18	Comments	• Only used in exceptional circumstances to provide additional information or clarification
19	Paid sick/ maternity/ parental/ compassionate	• Only completed if payment is insurable • When receiving payment, ROE is completed after all payments are exhausted (The last day payments apply is the last day for which paid)

	care/ family caregiver leave/ group wage loss indemnity payment	
20	Communication	• English or • French
21	Telephone Number	• Phone number of the person able to answer questions from Service Canada
22	Certification	Signature, printed name, and date of the person who is completing the ROE

ROE CHECKLIST

- Review all payroll information
- Review the dates and pay period type
- Review all insurable hours and only check if the numbers of hours included are according to the chart
- Review the number of pay periods needed for insurable earnings according to the chart
- Review information on Block 15B and 15C, if completed
- Review if insurable monies paid at termination are showing in Block 17 and in Block 15B, or pay period number one of Block 15C, if applicable
- Review for accuracy of all monies paid on separation or monies that will be paid while off in Block 17

Service Canada

If completing this form by hand: use a pen

EMPLOYER: SEE THE GUIDE - HOW TO COMPLETE THE RECORD OF EMPLOYMENT, IT IS
ALSO AVAILABLE ON THE WEB SITE AT: WWW.SERVICECANADA.GC.CA

Protected when completed - B

RECORD OF EMPLOYMENT (ROE)

1 SERIAL NO.	2 SERIAL NO. OF ROE AMENDED OR REPLACED	3 EMPLOYER'S PAYROLL REFERENCE NO.
E0000000		

4 EMPLOYER'S NAME AND ADDRESS	5 CRA's BUSINESS NO. (BN)
	6 PAY PERIOD TYPE
7 POSTAL CODE	8 SOCIAL INSURANCE NO.

9 EMPLOYEE'S NAME AND ADDRESS		D	M	Y
	10 FIRST DAY WORKED (ON FIRST DAY WORKED SINCE LAST ROE ISSUED)			
	11 LAST DAY FOR WHICH PAID			
	12 FINAL PAY PERIOD ENDING DATE			

13 OCCUPATION	14 EXPECTED DATE OF RECALL	D	M	Y
	☐ UNKNOWN ☐ NOT RETURNING			

15A TOTAL INSURABLE HOURS ACCORDING TO CHART ON REVERSE	16
.	REASON FOR ISSUING THIS ROE ► ENTER CODE [ ]

15B TOTAL INSURABLE EARNINGS ACCORDING TO CHART ON REVERSE	FOR FURTHER INFORMATION, CONTACT
$.	TELEPHONE NO. ► ( )

15C ONLY COMPLETE IF THERE HAS BEEN A PAY PERIOD WITH NO INSURABLE EARNINGS. COMPLETE ACCORDING TO CHART ON REVERSE.

P.P.	INSURABLE EARNINGS	P.P.	INSURABLE EARNINGS	P.P.	INSURABLE EARNINGS
1		2		3	
4		5		6	
7		8		9	
10		11		12	
13		14		15	
16		17		18	
19		20		21	
22		23		24	
25		26		27	

17 ONLY COMPLETE IF PAYMENTS OR BENEFITS (OTHER THAN REGULAR PAY) PAID IN OR IN ANTICIPATION OF THE FINAL PAY PERIOD OR PAYABLE AT A LATER DATE.

A - VACATION PAY	B - STATUTORY HOLIDAY PAY FOR				
$.	D	M	Y	$	.
				$	.
				$	.

C - OTHER MONIES (SPECIFY)

	$	.
	$	.
	$	.

19 ONLY COMPLETE IF PAID SICK/MATERNITY/PARENTAL LEAVE, OR GROUP WAGE LOSS INDEMNITY PAYMENT (AFTER THE LAST DAY WORKED).

PAYMENT START DATE			AMOUNT	
D	M	Y	$.	☐ PER DAY ☐ PER WEEK

20 COMMUNICATION PREFERRED IN	21 TELEPHONE NO.
☐ ENGLISH ☐ FRENCH	( )

18 COMMENTS

22 I AM AWARE THAT IT IS AN OFFENCE TO MAKE FALSE ENTRIES AND HEREBY CERTIFY THAT ALL STATEMENTS ON THIS FORM ARE TRUE.

	D	M	Y
SIGNATURE OF ISSUER			
NAME OF ISSUER (please print)	DATE		

ENTER CODE

- A SHORTAGE OF WORK
- B STRIKE OR LOCKOUT
- C RETURN TO SCHOOL
- D ILLNESS OR INJURY
- E QUIT
- F MATERNITY
- G RETIREMENT
- H WORK SHARING
- J APPRENTICE TRAINING
- M DISMISSAL
- N LEAVE OF ABSENCE
- P PARENTAL
- Z COMPASSIONATE CARE
- K OTHER EXPLAIN IN THE COMMENTS SECTION

PART 2 (BLUE) MUST BE SENT TO SERVICE CANADA P.O. BOX 9000 BATHURST, N.B. E2A1 A 3

Canada

Service Canada delivers Human Resources and Skills Development Canada programs and services for the Government of Canada.

EMPLOYEE'S COPY
*(See reverse) PART 1
Formulaire disponible en français.

INS-2106-01-10E

14. YEAR-END

T4 Slip & T4 Summary

Generally, you need to fill out a T4 slip if you are an employer (resident **or** non-resident) and you paid your employees employment income, commissions, taxable allowances and benefits, fishing income, or any other remuneration.
As an employer the following is mandatory:

- Report the income and deductions on the T4 slips that you will send to the CRA. To do this, fill out the T4 slips, Statement of Remuneration Paid. If you file on paper, also include the related T4 Summary, Summary of Remuneration Paid.
- File the T4 Summary, together with the related T4 slips, on or before the last day of February following the information about the filing methods you can use.
- Give employees their T4 slips on or before the last day of February following the calendar year to which the slips apply.
- Keep your paper and electronic records for six years after the year to which they relate.

Employers can be penalized $25 per day late, with a minimum penalty of $100 and a maximum penalty of $7,500. See link at bottom, to Canada Revenue Agency (CRA) page regarding penalty.
A T4 slip must be completed for everyone who received remuneration during the year if:

- CPP/QPP contributions, EI premiums, income tax, or Quebec PPIP premiums had to be deducted from the remuneration, or

- The remuneration was more than $500

REPORTING TAXABLE GROUP TERM LIFE INSURANCE BENEFITS

Report the benefit for **current employees and employees who are on a leave of absence** (such as maternity leave) in Box 14, "Employment Income", and in the "Other Information" area under Code **40** at the bottom of the employee's T4 slip.

For former employees or retirees, report the benefit on a T4A slip using Code **119** in the "Other Information" area, if it is more than $25. An exception to the $500 limit is when employees are provided with taxable group term life insurance benefits. In this case, for T4s must always be prepared, even if the total remuneration paid in the calendar year is less than $500.

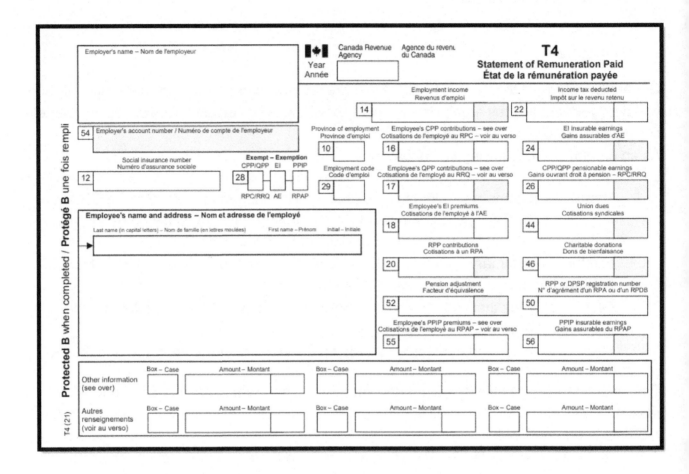

Report these amounts on your tax return.

14 – Employment income – Enter on line 10100.

16 – Employee's CPP contributions – See lines 30800 and 22215 in your tax guide.

17 – Employee's QPP contributions – See lines 30800 and 22215 in your tax guide.

18 – Employee's EI premiums – See line 31200 in your tax guide.

20 – RPP contributions – Includes past service contributions. See line 20700 in your tax guide.

22 – Income tax deducted – Enter on line 43700.

39 – Security options deduction 110(1)(d) – Enter on line 24900.

41 – Security options deduction 110(1)(d.1) – Enter on line 24900.

42 – Employment commissions – Enter on line 10120. This amount is already included in box 14.

43 – Canadian Armed Forces personnel and police deduction – Enter on line 24400. This amount is already included in box 14.

44 – Union dues – Enter on line 21200.

46 – Charitable donations.

52 – Pension adjustment – Enter on line 20600.

55 – Provincial parental insurance plan (PPIP) – Residents of Quebec, see line 31205 in your tax guide. Residents of provinces or territories other than Quebec, see line 31200 in your tax guide.

66 – Eligible retiring allowances – See line 13000 in your tax guide.

67 – Non-eligible retiring allowances – See line 13000 in your tax guide.

74 – Past service contributions for 1989 or earlier years while a contributor

75 – Past service contributions for 1989 or earlier years while not a contributor – See line 20700 in your tax guide.

77 – Workers' compensation benefits repaid to the employer – Enter on line 22900.

78 – Fishers – Gross income	See Form T2121.
79 – Fishers – Net partnership amount	**Do not** enter on line 10100.
80 – Fishers – Shareperson amount	

81 – Placement or employment agency workers	Gross income
82 – Taxi drivers and drivers of other passenger-carrying vehicles	See Form T2125. **Do not** enter on line 10100.
83 – Barbers or hairdressers	

85 – Employee-paid premiums for private health services plans – See line 33099 in your tax guide.

87 – Emergency services volunteer exempt amount – See "Emergency services volunteers" at line 10100, and the information at lines 31220 and 31240 in your tax guide.

71 – Indian (exempt income) – Employment	See Form T90. **Do not** enter this amount on line 10100 or lines 13499 to 14300.
88 – Indian (exempt income) – Self employed	

Do not report these amounts on your tax return. For Canada Revenue Agency use only.
(Amounts in boxes 30, 32, 34, 36, 38, 40, 57, 58, 59, 60, and 86 are already included in box 14.)

30 – Board and lodging

31 – Special work site

32 – Travel in a prescribed zone

33 – Medical travel assistance

34 – Personal use of employer's automobile or motor vehicle

36 – Interest-free and low-interest loans

38 – Security options benefits

40 – Other taxable allowances and benefits

57 – Employment Income – March 15 to May 9, 2020

58 – Employment Income – May 10 to July 4, 2020

59 – Employment Income – July 5 to August 29, 2020

60 – Employment Income – August 30 to September 26, 2020

69 – Indian (exempt income) – Non-eligible retiring allowances

86 – Security options election

Privacy Act, personal information bank numbers CRA PPU 005 and CRA PPU 047

T2200 – DECLARATION OF CONDITIONS OF EMPLOYMENT

The employee may be able to claim certain employment expenses on their <u>income tax and benefit return</u> if, under the contract of employment, the employee had to pay for the expenses in question.

EXAMPLES

- The company allows the employee personal use of motor vehicle for business and pay him a monthly motor vehicle allowance to pay for the operating expenses and you include the allowance in the employee's employment income as a taxable benefit.
  OR
- You have a formal telework arrangement with your employee that allows this employee to work at home. The employee pays for the expenses of this workspace on their own.

Reference:

T2200 Form

https://www.canada.ca/en/revenue-agency/services/forms-publications/forms/t2200.html

T2200s Form

https://www.canada.ca/en/revenue-agency/services/forms-publications/forms/t2200s.html

For additional information on Home Office Expense for Employees, go to

https://www.canada.ca/en/revenue-agency/services/tax/individuals/topics/about-your-tax-return/tax-return/completing-a-tax-return/deductions-credits-expenses/line-22900-other-employment-expenses/work-space-home-expenses.html?utm_campaign=not-applicable&utm_medium=vanity-url&utm_source=canada-ca_cra-home-workspace-expenses

A signed **Form T2200**, Declaration of Conditions of Employment, is given to employees so they can deduct employment expenses from their income.

By signing the form, you are only certifying that the employee met the conditions of employment and **had to pay for** the expenses under their employment contract.

For your 2020, 2021, or 2022 tax return, there are two options:

Temporary flat rate method		Detailed method

Temporary flat rate method

Applies to:

- ✔ eligible employees working from home in 2020, 2021, or 2022 due to the COVID-19 pandemic

With this method:

- ✔ you can claim $2 for each day you worked from home in 2020, 2021, or 2022 due to the COVID-19 pandemic
- ✔ you can claim up to a maximum per year of $400 in 2020 and up to $500 in 2021 and 2022
- ✔ your employer is not required to complete and sign Form T2200
- ✔ you are not required to keep documents to support your claim

Detailed method

Applies to:

- ✔ eligible employees working from home in 2020, 2021, or 2022 due to the COVID-19 pandemic
- ✔ eligible employees required to work from home

With this method:

- ✔ you can claim the actual amounts you paid, supported by documents
- ✔ you must have a completed and signed Form T2200S / Form T2200 from your employer

The T4 Summary provides summary information of total earnings for all employees. It also provides the summary total of contributions for CPP, EI and income tax that CRA is expecting the employer to submit.

15. PAYROLL ACCOUNTING

Journal Entry

A Payroll Journal is the form used to record gross earnings, deductions, and net earnings for all workers.

An employee's earning record is a form that records the cumulative totals of the employee's individual earnings and deductions for the year.

This is how the company monitors expenses and liabilities and budgets can be produced from the journal entries.

ACCOUNT	INCREASED BY	DECREASED BY
Assets	Debit	Credit
Expenses	Debit	Credit
Liabilities	Credit	Debit
Equity	Credit	Debit
Revenue	Credit	Debit

Basic Principles

Fundamental Canadian Payroll Administration

Journal Entry:

	Record Expense and Payroll Liabilities		
Date	Description	Debit	Credit
6/30/2023	Salary Expenses	$ 22,412.00	
	CPP Expense	$ 805.91	
	EI Expense	$ 753.05	
	WCB Expense	$ 515.48	
	Group Life Insurance Expense	$ 183.70	
	Employer CPP Payable		$ 805.91
	Employee EI Payable		$ 753.05
	Group Life Insurance Payable		$ 183.70
	WCB Payable		$ 515.48
	Employee CPP Payable		$ 805.91
	Employee EI Payable		$ 537.89
	Group Life Insurance Payable		$ 183.70
	Employee Pension Deduction		$ 705.59
	Income Tax Payable		$ 4,109.25
	Net Pay Payable		$ 16,069.66
		$ 24,670.14	$ 24,670.14

APPENDIX

Code of Professional Conduct

Professional

- Carry out their duties and responsibilities in a manner consistent with this Code and will strive to enhance the image of the Institute and its Members.
- Comply with the By-laws and the Code of Professional Conduct of the Institute as amended from time to time, and with any order or resolution of the Board or its committees under the By-laws.
- Act in the interest of employees, employers and interested third parties, and shall be prepared to sacrifice their self-interest to do so.
- Avoid conflicts of interest.
- Not make public statements or comments which may be interpreted as representing the Institute or its views, except when authorized to act as an official spokesperson.
- Notify the Institute of any breach of the Code by another Member, or any other situation of which the Member has sufficient knowledge which appears to put in doubt the competence, reputation or integrity of Members.
- Not issue a communication on any payroll information, whether for publication or not, when the information is prepared in a manner which might tend to be misleading. It is recognized that, under exceptional circumstances, compliance with this rule may place a Member in a difficult position in relation to the Member's employer. Nevertheless, it is a breach of professional duty if the Member becomes associated with any letter, report, statement, or representation which the Member knows, or ought to know, is false or misleading.
- Employ their technical expertise with due professional care and judgment

Community

- Have a fundamental responsibility to act with trustworthiness, integrity and objectivity.
- Not permit their name to be used with, participate in, or provide services to, any activity which they know, or which a reasonably prudent person would believe to be unprofessional or unlawful.
- Not discriminate against a person for any reason, and shall adhere to the guidelines as set out in the Canadian Charter of Rights and Freedom.
- Report to the Professional Conduct Committee any situation the Member has sufficient professional knowledge of and which the Member thinks may be detrimental to the Institute and its Members.

Authoritative Knowledge

- Respect personal and confidential relationships that may arise in business or professional activities as defined by privacy legislation, company policy and/or professional practice.
- Not disclose or use any confidential information concerning the affairs of any employee, former employee, employer or former employer except as described in this section.
- Disclose the employer's or employee's affairs: (a) where disclosure is compelled by a process of law or by a statute; or (b) where such information is required to be disclosed by the Professional Conduct Committee and the Board of Directors of the Institute in the proper exercise of their duties, unless such disclosure shall contravene the applicable Privacy Legislation of the jurisdiction the infraction takes place.
- A Member is not prohibited from disclosing the employer's or employee's affairs: (a) where properly acting in the course of the duties incumbent on a Member; or (b) where a Member becomes aware of apparent or suspected unprofessional activity. Before making such a disclosure, a Member should obtain advice from senior management within their organization in accordance with the policies and procedures of that organization, and then, if necessary, seek the advice of outside legal counsel as to the Member's duties and obligations as a member of the Institute subject to this code of Professional Conduct. A Member so doing shall not be in violation of this Rule regarding confidentiality by reason only of the seeking or following of such legal advice or reporting.
- Members who handle money or other property in trust shall do so in accordance with the terms of the trust and the general law relating to trusts. These Members shall maintain such records as are necessary to account properly for the money or other property.
- In accordance with the policies established by the Institute, a Member who holds a National Payroll Institute designation shall maintain a professional standing by participating in Continuing Professional Education (CPE) as defined by the Board of Directors.
- Not be associated with information which the Member knows, or ought to know, to be false or misleading, whether by statement or omission.
- Immediately disclose any material discrepancy that becomes known to the Member concerning payroll information on which the Member has issued a communication, or with which the Member is associated.

Enforcement

A Member shall be subject to disciplinary action under the Discipline Process of the Institute for any offence which constitutes a breach of professional conduct.

A Member who has been found guilty or granted an absolute or conditional discharge of any criminal or similar offence which may cast doubt as to that Member's honesty, integrity or professional competence, shall promptly inform the Institute in writing of the conviction, finding of guilt or discharge, as the case may be, when the right of appeal has been exhausted or expired. In such cases, the Member may be charged under the discipline process with professional misconduct by the Professional Conduct Committee. In such cases, satisfactory evidence of the conviction, finding of guilt or discharge issued by any competent court shall be sufficient evidence of the conviction and the perpetration of the offence.

Unprofessional or similar offences may include, but are not limited to, the following offences:

1. activity that is not consistent with the Academic Honesty Policy of the Institute;
2. fraud, theft, forgery or income tax evasion;
3. violation of the provisions of any securities legislation; or
4. any criminal or similar offence for conduct in, or related to, the Member's professional capacity, or for conduct in circumstances where there was reliance on the Member's Membership in, or affiliation with, the Institute.

The Chair of the Professional Conduct Committee will convene a meeting of the Committee to conduct an investigation. The Committee must submit a written report to the Chair within 30 days of completion of the investigation. The Professional Conduct Committee will recommend, through the Chair to the Board of Directors of the Institute, the recommended actions, which could include the suspension or termination of membership. The President will give the Board's decision to all parties within 30 days of receiving this report.

NPI : Code of Conduct

National Payroll Institute (NPI)

Reference: https://payroll.ca/who-we-are/code-of-professional-conduct

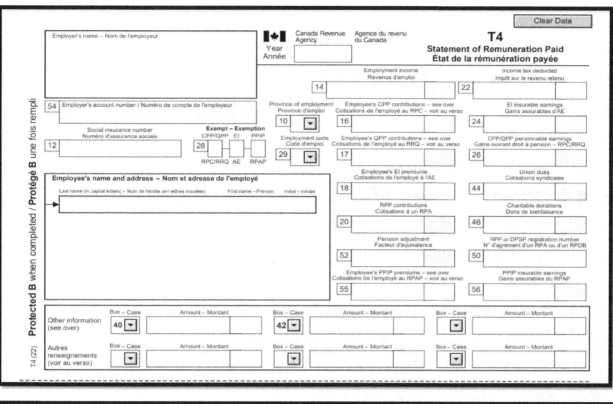

Report these amounts on your tax return.

14 – Employment income – Enter on line 10100.

16 – Employee's CPP contributions – See lines 30800 and 22215 in your tax guide.

17 – Employee's QPP contributions – See lines 30800 and 22215 in your tax guide.

18 – Employee's EI premiums – See line 31200 in your tax guide.

20 – RPP contributions – Includes past service contributions. See line 20700 in your tax guide.

22 – Income tax deducted – Enter on line 43700.

39 – Security options deduction 110(1)(d) – Enter on line 24900.

41 – Security options deduction 110(1)(d.1) – Enter on line 24900.

42 – Employment commissions – Enter on line 10120. This amount is already included in box 14.

43 – Canadian Armed Forces personnel and police deduction – Enter on line 24400. This amount is already included in box 14.

44 – Union dues – Enter on line 21200.

46 – Charitable donations.

52 – Pension adjustment – Enter on line 20600.

55 – Provincial parental insurance plan (PPIP) – Residents of Quebec, see line 31205 in your tax guide. Residents of provinces or territories other than Quebec, see line 31200 in your tax guide.

66 – Eligible retiring allowances – See line 13000 in your tax guide.

67 – Non-eligible retiring allowances – See line 13000 in your tax guide.

74 – Past service contributions for 1989 or earlier years while a contributor

75 – Past service contributions for 1989 or earlier years while not a contributor – See line 20700 in your tax guide.

77 – Workers' compensation benefits repaid to the employer – Enter on line 22900.

78 – Fishers – Gross income	
79 – Fishers – Net partnership amount	See Form T2121. **Do not** enter on line 10100.
80 – Fishers – Shareperson amount	

81 – Placement or employment agency workers	Gross income
82 – Taxi drivers and drivers of other passenger-carrying vehicles	See Form T2125. **Do not** enter on line 10100.
83 – Barbers or hairdressers	

85 – Employee-paid premiums for private health services plans – See line 33099 in your tax guide.

87 – Emergency services volunteer exempt amount – See "Emergency services volunteers" at line 10100, and the information at lines 31220 and 31240 in your tax guide.

69 – Indian (exempt income) – Non-eligible retiring allowances	See Form T90. **Do not** enter these amounts on line 10100, line 13000 or lines 13499 to 14300.
71 – Indian (exempt income) – Employment	
88 – Indian (exempt income) – Self employed	

Do not report these amounts on your tax return. For Canada Revenue Agency use only.
(Amounts in boxes 30, 32, 34, 36, 38, 40, 57, 58, 59, 60, and 86 are already included in box 14.)

30 – Board and lodging

31 – Special work site

32 – Travel in a prescribed zone

33 – Medical travel assistance

34 – Personal use of employer's automobile or motor vehicle

36 – Interest-free and low-interest loans

38 – Security options benefits

40 – Other taxable allowances and benefits

57 – Employment Income – March 15 to May 9, 2020

58 – Employment Income – May 10 to July 4, 2020

59 – Employment Income – July 5 to August 29, 2020

60 – Employment Income – August 30 to September 26, 2020

86 – Security options election

T4 (22)

References and Links

- Canadian Payroll Certification
- Payroll Overview – Employer Responsibilities
- Working in BC
- TD1 - Personal Tax Credit Returns
- T2200 - Declaration of Conditions of Employment
- T2200s Declaration of Conditions of Employment for Working at Home due to COVID-19
- Minimum Wage across Canada – *Payworks*
- Vacation Pay in British Columbia
- Statutory Holidays in Canada - *Payworks*
- Benefits and Allowance Chart – Canada Revenue Agency
- Canadian Pension Plan (CPP) – Canada Revenue Agency
- Employment Insurance (EI) – Canada Revenue Agency
- Personal Income Tax Rates – Canada Revenue Agency
- T4032BC Payroll Deduction Tables – CPP, EI and income tax deductions - BC
- Payroll Deduction Online Calculator (PDOC)
- How to complete the record of employment (ROE) form
- Filing the T4 Slip and T4 Summary

Payroll outsourcing

Payroll service outsourcing is an arrangement between the two companies where one company enters into a contract with another company to take care of its payroll services. It is an excellent alternative to in-house payroll.

It is also an efficient way to get professional help without worrying about giving any guidelines.

Fundamental Canadian Payroll Administration

Federal tax deductions
Effective January 1, 2022
Biweekly (26 pay periods a year)
Also look up the tax deductions in the provincial table

Pay From	Less than	CC 0	CC 1	CC 2	CC 3
1299	1315	175.50	92.45	85.45	71.40
1315	1331	177.75	94.65	87.65	73.65
1331	1347	179.95	96.90	89.90	75.85
1347	1363	182.20	99.10	92.10	78.10
1363	1379	184.40	101.35	94.35	80.30
1379	1395	186.65	103.55	96.55	82.55
1395	1411	188.85	105.80	98.80	84.75
1411	1427	191.10	108.00	101.00	87.00
1427	1443	193.30	110.25	103.25	89.20
1443	1459	195.55	112.45	105.45	91.45
1459	1475	197.75	114.70	107.70	93.65
1475	1491	200.00	116.90	109.90	95.90
1491	1507	202.20	119.15	112.15	98.10
1507	1523	204.45	121.35	114.35	100.35
1523	1539	206.65	123.60	116.60	102.55
1539	1555	208.90	125.80	118.80	104.80
1555	1571	211.10	128.05	121.05	107.00
1571	1587	213.35	130.25	123.25	109.25
1587	1603	215.55	132.50	125.50	111.45
1603	1619	217.80	134.70	127.70	113.70
1619	1635	220.00	136.95	129.95	115.90
1635	1651	222.25	139.15	132.15	118.15
1651	1667	224.45	141.40	134.40	120.35
1667	1683	226.70	143.60	136.60	122.60
1683	1699	228.90	145.85	138.85	124.80
1699	1715	231.15	148.05	141.05	127.05
1715	1731	233.35	150.30	143.30	129.25
1731	1747	235.60	152.50	145.50	131.50
1747	1763	237.80	154.75	147.75	133.70
1763	1779	240.05	156.95	149.95	135.95
1779	1795	242.25	159.20	152.20	138.15
1795	1811	244.50	161.40	154.40	140.40
1811	1827	246.70	163.65	156.65	142.60
1827	1843	248.95	165.85	158.85	144.85
1843	1859	251.15	168.10	161.10	147.05
1859	1875	253.40	170.30	163.30	149.30
1875	1891	255.60	172.55	165.55	151.50
1891	1907	257.85	174.75	167.75	153.75
1907	1923	260.05	177.00	170.00	155.95
1923	1939	262.30	179.25	172.25	158.20
1939	1955	265.40	182.35	175.35	161.30
1955	1971	268.50	185.45	178.45	164.40
1971	1987	271.60	188.55	181.55	167.50
1987	2003	274.70	191.65	184.65	170.65
2003	2019	277.85	194.75	187.75	173.75
2019	2035	280.95	197.85	190.85	176.85

Fundamental Canadian Payroll Administration

British Columbia provincial tax deductions
Effective January 1, 2022
Biweekly (26 pay periods a year)
Also look up the tax deductions in the federal table

Pay From	Less than	CC 0	CC 1	CC 2	CC 3
1511	1527	71.65	49.65	47.20	42.25
1527	1543	72.40	50.40	47.95	43.00
1543	1559	73.15	51.15	48.70	43.75
1559	1575	73.90	51.90	49.45	44.50
1575	1591	74.65	52.65	50.20	45.25
1591	1607	75.40	53.40	50.95	46.00
1607	1623	76.15	54.15	51.70	46.75
1623	1639	76.90	54.90	52.45	47.50
1639	1655	77.65	55.65	53.20	48.25
1655	1671	78.60	56.60	54.10	49.15
1671	1687	79.75	57.75	55.30	50.35
1687	1703	80.95	58.95	56.45	51.50
1703	1719	82.10	60.10	57.65	52.70
1719	1735	83.25	61.30	58.80	53.85
1735	1751	84.45	62.45	60.00	55.05
1751	1767	85.60	63.65	61.15	56.20
1767	1783	86.80	64.80	62.30	57.40
1783	1799	87.95	65.95	63.50	58.55
1799	1815	89.15	67.15	64.65	59.70
1815	1831	90.30	68.30	65.85	60.90
1831	1847	91.50	69.50	67.00	62.05
1847	1863	92.65	70.65	68.20	63.25
1863	1879	93.85	71.85	69.35	64.40
1879	1895	95.00	73.00	70.55	65.60
1895	1911	96.20	74.20	71.70	66.75
1911	1927	97.35	75.35	72.90	67.95
1927	1943	98.50	76.55	74.05	69.10
1943	1959	99.70	77.70	75.25	70.30
1959	1975	100.85	78.90	76.40	71.45
1975	1991	102.05	80.05	77.55	72.65
1991	2007	103.20	81.20	78.75	73.80
2007	2023	104.40	82.40	79.90	74.95
2023	2039	105.55	83.55	81.10	76.15
2039	2055	106.75	84.75	82.25	77.30
2055	2071	107.90	85.90	83.45	78.50
2071	2087	109.10	87.10	84.60	79.65
2087	2103	110.25	88.25	85.80	80.85
2103	2119	111.45	89.45	86.95	82.00
2119	2135	112.60	90.60	88.15	83.20
2135	2151	113.75	91.80	89.30	84.35
2151	2167	114.95	92.95	90.50	85.55
2167	2183	116.10	94.15	91.65	86.70
2183	2199	117.30	95.30	92.80	87.85
2199	2215	118.45	96.45	94.00	89.05
2215	2231	119.65	97.65	95.15	90.20

Made in the USA
Monee, IL
02 November 2024

69150458R00077